D0426114

Swish

Swish

MY QUEST TO BECOME THE GAYEST PERSON EVER

Joel Derfner

Broadway Books

New York

PUBLISHED BY BROADWAY BOOKS

Copyright © 2008 by Joel Derfner

All Rights Reserved

Published in the United States by Broadway Books,
an imprint of The Doubleday Broadway Publishing Group,
a division of Random House, Inc., New York.
www.broadwaybooks.com

BROADWAY BOOKS and its logo, a letter B bisected on the diagonal,
are trademarks of Random House, Inc.

The author and publisher gratefully acknowledge the following for the
right to reprint material in this book:
Petr Ginz (1928–1944)
Moon Landscape, 1942–1944
Pencil on paper
Collection of the Yad Vashem Art Museum, Jerusalem
Gift of Otto Ginz, Haifa

"Without You"
Written by Peter Ham and Tom Evans
©1970, 1999 (renewed) BUGHOUSE (ASCAP) O/B/O/ BUG MUSIC
LTD (PRS)
All Rights Reserved. Used by Permission.

Library of Congress Cataloging-in-Publication Data
Derfner, Joel.
    Swish : my quest to become the gayest person ever / by Joel
    Derfner. — 1st ed.
        p. cm.
    1. Derfner, Joel. 2. Gay men—United States—Biography.
3. Gay men—United States—Psychology. I. Title.
HQ75.8.D46A3 2008
306.76'62092—dc22
    [B]
                                2007049906

ISBN 978-0-7679-2430-6

PRINTED IN THE UNITED STATES OF AMERICA

10 9 8 7 6 5 4 3 2 1

First Edition

for Mike

CONTENTS

$\mathcal{I}$NTRODUCTION

A few years ago I wrote a book called *Gay Haiku*. Writing a book had never been a particular goal of mine, except for two weeks during the eighth grade, after I read Truman Capote's *Other Voices, Other Rooms;* my resulting desire to be an author lasted until I finished *Breakfast at Tiffany's,* at which point I realized it would be much more interesting to be a prostitute. But in 2003, as part of a fund-raiser for a theater company some friends of mine and I were starting, I wrote 49 haiku about all the bad dates I'd been going on and all the bad sex I'd been having since my boyfriend and I broke up. The haiku turned out well, so I wrote 20 more and sent the collection to an agent as a manuscript called *69 Gay Haiku*. She liked it and sent it to a publisher; he also liked it, but he said 69 haiku wasn't enough and 110 seemed like a more appropriate number. I was upset, not because the prospect of writing more haiku was so horrible, but because *69 Gay Haiku* was the only decent title I had ever come up with for anything and I was loath to discard it. I suggested the title *69 Gay Haiku Plus 41 More* but the reception with which this idea met was singularly unenthusiastic.

When the book appeared on shelves, however, I stopped being upset about the title because all of a sudden I got to tell people things like, "Sorry, Monday's no good for me, I'm having lunch with my publicist." (The only thing I've ever said more glamorous than this was, "Yes, I can meet you at your apartment for casual sex tomorrow morning, unless I have to go to Prague.") The fact that my publicist and I spent the entire lunch in question gushing about how vigorously we wanted to rip Chris Meloni's clothing off didn't matter in the least; what was important was that I could use her in a sentence. This was by far the best thing about becoming a published author.

The worst thing about becoming a published author was that, inexplicably, it did not make all my problems go away. Walking into Barnes & Noble and seeing my name on a book jacket was exciting, of course, but when I left the store the thought filling my head was not *Gee, now my life is perfect* but *Why didn't the cute cashier fall in love with me as I purchased my own book? Am I fat? Or could he just see that I'm a bad person?*

I spent a long time considering the possibilities. Perhaps the book had failed to make all my problems go away because it was too small? Too cute? Was it too pink? To do what it was supposed to do, did a book need more than seventeen syllables a page?

Finally I decided that the only solution was to write another, better book. For a while I toyed with the idea of a collection of light verse, amusing myself to no end producing nonpareils like:

> Ozzily Tozzily
> Wicked Witch Elphaba
> Spied on Miss Gale, feeling
> Down in the dumps.

> "Hmph," she remarked, somewhat
> Unfetishistically—
> "Long way to go for some
> Lousy red pumps."

However, I realized before long that if my aim was to produce a more dazzling book with wider appeal, *Gay Double Dactyls* was unlikely to do the trick. So I invited my editor for *Gay Haiku* to lunch (by which I mean I invited him to *buy me* lunch) and said, "I have to write another book for you to make all my problems go away, what do you want?"

"Well," he said, trying unsuccessfully to hide his consternation at my having ordered a meal composed entirely of partially hydrogenated fat, "there's that thing from your bio in *Gay Haiku* about trying to become the gayest person ever. I guess you could write a book about that." I agreed immediately, because our waiter had returned with the appetizers, and I am rendered so powerless in the face of mozzarella sticks that I would have said okay if my editor had suggested I write a book about scaling Mount Kilimanjaro in a bustle.

So when I got home, full of contentment and fried breaded cheese, I set about my task. Before the publication of *Gay Haiku,* panicked because my bio for the book jacket was late, I had scribbled down a paragraph that included the sentence "In an attempt to become the gayest person ever, he took up knitting and got a job as a step aerobics instructor." As far as the new book was concerned, those two achievements meant little in isolation, of course, but they were not my only credentials: I also wrote musical theater and cheered on the gay cheerleading squad and had had a lot of gay sex. Though I had a long way to go to reach the status of, say, J. Edgar Hoover, I felt nevertheless that I was starting from a position of strength.

My first task was to decide where to begin. Figuring *what the hell, sex sells,* I started writing about casual sex. This would be an easy topic, I knew, as I had a wealth of experience upon which to draw. I had to make up some names and a detail or three to fill the ever-widening gaps in my aging memory, but on the whole things were going swimmingly until I looked down at my computer screen and saw that I had started to write about Johnny Depp.

Please do not get the wrong (though breathtaking) idea. I have never had sex with Johnny Depp, at least not outside of REM sleep. But I had begun to explore an idea that wouldn't make sense unless I related a story about my childhood reaction to a television character played by that gentleman, and this story required me in turn to relate certain other stories about my childhood, and before I knew it I was writing something completely different from what I had set out to write, something that involved discussions of New Age bookstores and Miss Manners and the Ancien Régime.

Obviously, this would never do, so I decided to scrap the whole thing and start over. But as I reached for the delete key it occurred to me that, in fact, juxtaposing the anecdote about the Scottish guy's dirty talk with a disquisition on Marie Antoinette's executioners made me understand each of those two things in a slightly different, more interesting way than writing about either one of them alone. They felt connected under the surface.

"This is more complicated than I expected it to be," I complained to my boyfriend on the phone.

"What's wrong with that?" he asked.

"What's wrong with that is I started writing a sidesplittingly funny discussion of sex and I ended up discovering things about my own character, *that's* what's wrong with that," I snapped. Then I hung up and went on to the next chapter, which was about knitting, except that before long I realized that it was also about my mother.

This kept happening over and over again. I would start

writing about some stereotypically gay pursuit in which I was involved and learn along the way that my interest in it came not just from my being gay but also from some deeper need it met. I undertook new gay projects in furtherance of my quest—I went to gay summer camp, I became a go-go boy, I married Liza Minnelli—but even these turned out to sound unexpected echoes with other, seemingly irrelevant, parts of my life.

This introduction used to end with a cute bit about how the subtitle of this book was a lie, because I wasn't actually on a quest to become the gayest person ever, because first of all who would do that with R——— S——— still in the public eye, but I was told I couldn't use R——— S———'s real name, which took all the humor out of it. Then my editor pointed out that in any case to introduce the book this way was a facile piece of chicanery that sidestepped the truth. I thanked him for the critique and pointed out that he was fat and that no one loved him.

But upon reflection I think that my editor was right. It's not that my quest to become the gayest person ever was a lie; it's that writing about my quest to become the gayest person ever led me to realize that I was actually on a quest to become myself.

I told this to my boyfriend, who is a psychiatrist, and he said, "Well, that makes sense. You definitely have some narcissistic traits."

"Don't touch me," I said.

There is no question but that my quest to become the gayest person ever has failed. I take one look at the plays of Oscar Wilde or the dialogues of Plato or the headlines about the Republican-Politician-Arrested-for-Solicitation-in-the-Men's-Room of the Week and I want to hang my head in shame. But what I'm hoping is that, like Columbus landing on

San Salvador, I've reached a new world: a land of vistas to explore, horizons to pursue, indigenous peoples to subjugate. And now that all my problems are going to go away, I'm all set to start doing those things, just as soon as I'm done having lunch with my publicist, because in last night's episode of *Law & Order: SVU* Chris Meloni took his shirt off and so she and I have a lot to discuss.

P.S.: If I've dated you or slept with you and any of the anecdotes in this book seem to be about you, they're not. They're about somebody else. You were divine.

P.P.S.: I know I said the same thing in the introduction to my last book, but this time I mean it.

Swish

ON KNITTING

*T*he two Englishmen were staring at the half-finished glove in my hands, aghast. "What is *that*?" the short one asked. "I know it's a mess," I rushed to apologize. I was lying. It was not a mess; it was perfect. But I had just arrived from the airport and I didn't want to offend them, as they were my hosts while I was in town for a small theater's production of a musical to which I had composed the score. The couple continued to stare in reproving silence at the work in my lap. "I've never done a glove before," I continued desperately, "and the fingers are trickier than I expected, and they—"

"No!" the tall one interrupted, his voice quick with dismay. "It's not that. It's that you're *knitting*. Men don't knit, young people don't knit. Knitting is . . . something your *grandmother* does!"

My mother's mother was a raging alcoholic who had been married seven or nine times (depending on whether you counted the annulment and the common-law bigamy), including once to a member of the House Un-American Activities Committee and once to a French royalist arms smuggler, so I felt I could safely assert that knitting was not a pastime she had ever enjoyed. "Besides," I said defensively, "knitting is very fashionable in New York these days."

"Well, this isn't New York," the short one retorted, but something in my face must have inspired pity.

"All right," said the tall one grudgingly. "Just as long as nobody sees you doing it in public."

But it was already too late, as the tube ride from the airport had been a long one. To mollify them, I put the knitting away, and then we had sex. It was more than satisfactory, as far as that sort of thing goes, but I still didn't trust them. What kind of people would disapprove of the manufacture of a pair of beautiful cable-stitch gloves, no matter by whose hand?

My friend Cynthia tried to teach me to knit in college. She was a good instructress, but no matter how relentlessly supportive she was I always ended up feeling as if Tomás de Torquemada had taken an especial interest in my hands. It became clear to me very soon that I would never create a garment. I was destined to buy my clothes forever from The Gap. In fact, I thought as I massaged my cramped, searing palms, I would never create anything; I would only be a barnacle on the seedy consumerist underbelly of humanity, sucking up resources and contributing nothing but the occasional second-rate witticism.

But years later, after my boyfriend Tom broke up with me, I thought, *Why not try again?* In the last two years, twenty-nine weeks, and four days not that I was counting or anything, I had mastered utterly the legerdemain required for the illusion that I was in a healthy relationship. What difficulty could winding pieces of string around each other pose my nimble fingers now?

So I signed up for a course at a yarn store called Gotta Knit. There were six students in the class: five women between the ages of forty-five and fifty-five and me. On the first night the teacher, a young woman named Mindy, put six balls of acrylic yarn on the table and told each of us to pick one. Five of the balls were pink and one was purple; I wanted the purple ball of yarn more than I ever wanted anything in my life, including the time I was at a charity auction and lost a bidding war for an autographed photo of Ralph Macchio and snuck in during dinner and stole it and left cash on the table to match the winning bid. But in Gotta Knit I held back out of politeness and somebody else swooped in and pounced on the purple ball, leaving me with one of the dumb pink ones just like everybody else. My immediate impulse was to push my rival out the window, but I did not want to go to prison—the uniform would almost certainly not be in my colors—so instead I seethed with rage and imagined clawing her eyes out or sending her anthrax in the mail.

Mindy explained the basics and before long we were all knitting miniature sweaters furiously. Or at least *I* was knitting furiously; I have no idea what emotional state suffused the others, but I wanted to win. I wanted to crush the yarn; I wanted to beat it into submission.

Soon enough, however, my hands began to feel that familiar, excruciating tightness and I knew I would be unable to continue if I didn't find a way to relieve it. When I asked Mindy for help, she bent over, performed a piece of prestidigitation I couldn't follow at all, and lo and behold! the yarn was wrapped around my fingers in a different direction.

"Your hands should stop hurting now," she said, "and your stitches will also be a lot looser." The agony spiking through my palms subsided almost right away, and the piece became much easier to work with, weaving effortlessly around itself.

Mindy asked us why we were taking the class. I opened my mouth to speak, but "My boyfriend just broke up with me and I need something to do with my hands other than Google him obsessively" seemed too revealing, so instead I muttered something about always having wanted to learn but never having had the opportunity.

"My mother taught me how, forty years ago, but I forgot," said one of the other class members.

"My mother wouldn't teach me," replied another. "She said there were more useful things for a girl to learn."

"You, too? Mine said she was going to teach me but she never got around to it."

"My mother didn't knit at all, and I was so jealous of Sally Pierce next door, because her mother taught her how. So I finally decided to do something about it."

We all turned to the last woman, the bitch who had stolen my purple yarn, to see what she would tell us about her mother. "My boyfriend just broke up with me," she said, "and I need something to do with my hands other than Google him obsessively." I dropped my next five stitches and it took Mindy twenty minutes to show me how to pick them up again.

My mother did not knit. She did not quilt, or crochet, or needlepoint; crafts of all kinds were anathema to her. I took a different attitude, at least in my formative years. At some point in my childhood I came home from school with a birthday present I'd made for her, a mobile from which I had hung stuffed misshapen felt hearts in every color of the rainbow. I would have stitched her a sampler that said YOUR SON WILL GROW UP TO KNOW ALL THE WORDS TO "IT'S RAINING MEN," but I had yet to discover disco, so the stuffed hearts were the best I could do. If she was unsettled by the gift she didn't show it; it dangled brightly in an upstairs window for months.

However, though she disdained handiwork, my mother was nevertheless a whiz, when circumstances required, with the more consistent sewing machine. At the age of eight I was cast as Helios, the sun, in my school's musical retelling of the myth of Persephone. I got home from practice one day to find my mother smoking, her brow wrinkled in concern as she read the sheet of paper upon which were written the school's costume instructions. She did not show me the instructions but they doubtless called for bedsheets and flip-flops. "I don't know exactly what they mean by this," she said, which meant "These people are morons and should be put down like dogs; I'd shoot them myself but I have more important things to do with my time." Then she threw the instructions away, went to her Singer, and actually made me a costume *out of gold lamé.*

It was in this costume, complete with laurels of gold tinsel—what was she *thinking?*—that I sang to Demeter, played by our music teacher, about her daughter's dark and chthonic fate. After the curtain call my mother hugged me and my little brother (who had played Hades' gardener) and told us how proud she was and took us out for ice cream. In between spoonfuls of Rocky Road I asked her the question that had stumped me at school during recess earlier in the day. "Would you rather," I said, "go blind or deaf?"

After a few moments' thought she said, "It would be really hard not to be able to see anything, but I'd rather go blind, because if I went deaf I would never be able to hear my children's voices again."

Would that I had understood the gift I was being given.

At the end of the first class at Gotta Knit, we had all made good progress on our miniature sweaters. I went home and by the next afternoon I had finished all the pieces, including the front with the difficult low-cut neck. The following morning I waited outside the store for two hours until it opened and then I bought needles and yarn to knit my friend Rob a scarf in a reverse rib pattern with a deliciously soft blue-green alpaca.

The class lasted for another three weeks. There are essentially only two stitches in knitting, however—knit and purl, each of which is more or less the reverse of the other—and so the remaining sessions were devoted to the myriad ways in which these two stitches can be manipulated. I learned increasing, decreasing, ribbing, and cabling. I also learned to say things like "a deliciously soft blue-green alpaca." I began to shop for yarn as if I were at a wine tasting. "This yarn has supercilious undertones, masked by a patina of enthusiasm," I would say to the woman behind the counter. "This yarn is $10.95 a ball," she would reply.

Rob's scarf reached its full six-foot length in a matter of days, and I was hooked. I started knitting everywhere. I knitted on the subway. I knitted at my job. I knitted during the sermon in church.

It is not, of course, Jewish custom to attend church, but

I needed the money. In New York, as in many other large metropolitan areas, church choirs tend to be made up not of parishioners but of professional singers, irrespective of faith, so as to ensure the high quality of the music. I've worked at a number of New York churches; at the time I learned to knit I was singing at the Church of St. Mary the Virgin in Times Square, known around town as Smoky Mary's because of all the incense. I was thrilled to get a job there, not just because Smoky Mary's has no acoustic peer in the Western Hemisphere, but also because the congregation has historically been composed almost exclusively of men who know the difference between beige and taupe. This is the church at which Tallulah Bankhead is reputed to have caught the attention of the thurifer as he walked down the aisle swinging the censer and said, "Darling, I love your dress, but your purse is on fire."

The most exciting thing about singing at St. Mary's, however, was that the choir sat above and behind the congregation, which meant that nobody could see us. And so, when we weren't singing, we were doing the crossword, flirting shamelessly with one another—at least the tenors and basses were—and, now, knitting. Whoever invented the phrase "preaching to the choir" clearly had no idea what goes on when the antiphon is over and the music folders come down. The choristers at Smoky Mary's were abetted in our delinquency by the sound system, which consisted essentially of tin cans connected by dental floss, so that we could never hear anything the priests down below were saying. It's certainly possible that the sermons preached at St. Mary's would have uplifted my spirit and saved my soul had I been able to hear them, but after five minutes of intense, strained focus at my first Sunday-morning service there, I decided that blissful ignorance was preferable to an inner ear injury, and (since I had not yet learned to knit) opened *Mansfield Park*.

The music was a different matter. The walls of Smoky Mary's are made of stone instead of concrete, so sound bounces off them and comes back twice as rich and clear—and then hits the opposite walls and reaches the congregation's ears quadruply refined. Singing in that room is as effortless as breathing; you open your mouth and your voice pours out like water from a jar. Even the worst music becomes beautiful in that space, and the best can fill you with the desire for what is known in Hebrew as *tikkun olam*, the healing of the world. "As truly as God is our Father," we sang one Sunday in a gorgeous setting of a text by fourteenth-century mystic Julian of Norwich, "so just as truly is He our Mother. In our Father, God Almighty, we have our being; in our merciful Mother we are remade and restored. Our fragmented lives are knit together, and by giving and yielding ourselves, through grace, to the Holy Spirit, we are made whole." And then the echo died, and the priest started muttering, "Umpho flumpish klizmar," and I picked up my size-eight needles.

In our merciful Mother we are remade and restored? I thought as I went back to my first attempt at working in two colors. *Our fragmented lives are knit together?* Their god may be a lie, but if he's a cross-dresser with good hobbies he can't be all bad.

It was around the time I began my first hat that people started speaking to me on the subway. People had been speaking *about*

me on the subway from the moment I first pulled out my yarn on the uptown A train, and I loved it. There is no joy quite like that of hearing people whisper, "What's he knitting, it's so complicated, I used to be able to crochet but I would never have the patience to do something like that" in the hushed tones ordinarily reserved for apparitions of the Virgin Mary in food. But being spoken *to* turned out to be an almost invariably unpleasant proposition. No matter how mellifluous the voice that asked, "What are you knitting?" when I looked up I was bound to see someone either wearing a funny beret decorated with plastic flowers or carrying a portfolio brimming with tattered, close-written proofs of the two-shooter theory.

On the crosstown bus one evening a boy of eight or nine leaned forward and spoke to me from across the aisle. "What are you knitting?" he piped.

In addition to dreading that question, I also hate children. One would think that these two facts in combination should have inspired me on this cold December night to a stony silence, but I was feeling generous. "A baby blanket," I answered condescendingly, glad to be able to broaden the waif's horizons.

He sat back in his seat. "I just finished a scarf," he said primly, "in fisherman's rib. Now I'm working on a Fair Isle sweater, but I have to hurry if I'm going to finish it in time for Christmas."

Once I recovered my equilibrium, I responded. "That sounds terrific. Good luck."

What I wanted to say was, *"Does your mother know how gay you are?"*

It was in the summer after ninth grade that I came out to my-self, and, a week later, to my parents. When my mother said she wanted to talk to me after lunch, I knew she was going to ask me whether I had an eating disorder (I had been eating noth-ing but grilled cheese sandwiches for the last several weeks, and not very many of them). So when I went up to her room to talk to her, I was relieved when all she said was, "Joel, are you gay?"

"Oh," I said casually. "Yeah." The library books I'd left on the kitchen table must have clued her in; it would be difficult to misinterpret a title like *Now That You Know: A Parents' Guide to Understanding Homosexuality*.

Not a muscle in my mother's face moved. "What do you mean, *yeah?*" she asked in a voice that could have flash-frozen the population of Zambia.

Obviously I had given her the wrong answer, but I couldn't for the life of me figure out how. She and my father were civil rights workers, after all; they had committed their lives to *tikkun olam*. He had won his first Supreme Court voting-rights case at the age of thirty, and she, despite never having finished college, was the author of the law that forces corporations and government agencies to pay the lawyers of the people whose civil rights they've violated, which law is now the only reason anybody can afford to be a civil rights lawyer. Two weeks after the 1970 massacre at Kent State University of students protesting the American invasion of Cambodia, a similar massacre took place at Jackson State College in Missis-sippi. Nobody cared about this one, though, because the stu-dents killed were black. But my mother, who lived nearby, found an audiotape of the gunfire, which lasted for a horrify-ing thirty seconds, and convinced a local radio station to play it nonstop for an entire day and night. Then she organized a march on the governor's mansion in which people carried signs offering friendly criticisms like GOD WILL GIVE YOU BLOOD TO DRINK.

Furthermore, my parents stayed true to their principles even when they themselves were the wrongdoers. When I was five, I picketed my house, hoping to be allowed to eat breakfast before getting dressed rather than after. I marched back and forth on our porch, carrying a sign that said BREKFAST FIRST DRESSED LATER; since my parents didn't cross picket lines, and since the front door was the only way into and out of the house, they were trapped inside until they acceded to my demand.

So, if my mother had built her entire life around protecting the rights of the disenfranchised, no matter the price to herself, what problem could she possibly have with a little flouncing here and there? I cast about for other explanations. Perhaps it was my sloppy diction to which she objected. I tried again. "I mean . . . yes, I'm gay?"

The thrust of the story will be familiar to many who have told their parents they're not straight. My mother and father said they didn't mind if I was gay—they just didn't want me to make up my mind so soon. They tried therefore to eliminate all gay influences from my life; unfortunately, they did this by coming up with prohibitions so stupid they were embarrassing. I wasn't allowed to wear bow ties. I wasn't allowed to write in green ink. I wasn't allowed to compose sonnets to boys (though given the quality of the verse I had been writing, that one was more than fair). They forbade me to see the one gay person I knew, the screamingly homosexual owner of Charleston's best chocolate store. I regularly told them I was going to the library and went to see him instead, and when they found out they grounded me for a year—not for being gay, they insisted, but for lying to them. I tried desperately to explain that none of this was going to dampen my enthusiasm for opera or my interest in the minor works of E. M. Forster, but the murky cloud of their hope was impenetrable.

It would probably have dissipated on its own in good time if my mother hadn't also been dying of juvenile diabetes. For a long time she had kept the disease at bay with panache, decorating her portable IV pole as a tree one Hallowe'en when I was six or seven and showing up at a party as Johnny Appleseed. By the time I was in junior high, however, her struggle had become more difficult; the first time she was carried out of the house to an ambulance in the middle of the night screaming that she was being ripped apart, I sat on the floor of my room paying very close attention to the model dragon I was gluing together until my uncle, her brother, knocked on my door frame and told me she was probably going to live. I thought that if I looked at him I might discover he was just as frightened as I was, so I kept my eyes on the dragon's right hind claw, which with a great deal of concentration I finally attached successfully.

After tenth grade my de jure grounding was over, but soon enough my father was spending all his time in Alabama arguing a desegregation case for which he was later named Trial Lawyer of the Year by the Trial Lawyers for Public Justice; the case lasted a year, during which period I had to spend all *my* time taking care of my terminally ill mother and my younger brother, who had heard from Jamie Adams that Allison Orson had said I was a lesbian, and wanted to know what that meant. I still resented my mother deeply, because she kept doing things like collecting any mail that came for me, asking me if it was from people she'd want me to be in contact with, and throwing it away if I told her it wasn't. It didn't occur to me to lie, and since we had moved to a house with a back door a picket wouldn't have done any good, so all the mail from kids on the pen-pal list I'd gotten from the gay youth hotline went unread into the trash. The return address on one letter was so illegible that it was impossible for me to tell who had sent it. My mother, in a backward baseball cap because she hadn't been well enough to go to the stylist in months, opened the envelope and proceeded to read me passages from my own mail, grimacing at the expressions of affection contained therein. I sat frozen in helpless fury before her until I realized the letter was from a straight friend I had met at summer camp. At this point she allowed me to go and read the rest in my room, where I sat on my bed and turned the pages and trembled with hatred.

I spun elaborate fantasies in which I would confront her, implacable in my oratory, and reduce her to a quivering pudding capable only of tearful attempts at reconciliation, which I would ruthlessly spurn. But when your mother gets out of her wheelchair and crawls up the stairs in her nightgown on hands and knees bleeding from diabetic neuropathy, gaily pretending that she has simply found a particularly invigorating new form of exercise, and all you can do, since your father is five hundred miles away saving the world, is make her a rum and Coke with enough Bacardi to knock out a rhinoceros, it becomes difficult to tell her that when she rejected your sexuality she hurt your *feelings*.

Almost twenty years later, her reasons for reacting so badly to my coming out remain shrouded in mystery. Perhaps she had some traumatic experience as a child—more traumatic than all the rest of her experiences as a child, which, given my much-married grandmother's propensity to cruelty, is really saying something—that predisposed her to rabidity. My great-great-uncle was purportedly the queeniest queen ever to queen his way down Queensville Pike; possibly she blamed herself for passing those genetic tendencies along. After she died I was looking through some of her papers and found a letter in which she seemed to come close to confessing an attraction to a woman who had lived around the corner from us when I was five. Maybe she was just jealous that I could say it and she couldn't.

Eventually, after I'd run out of friends to make scarves and hats for, I decided I needed to move on to something more challenging. I was sort of dating a guy named Mike; he was about to move to Boston for a year, so I resolved to knit him a pair of warm socks. We'd been seeing each other for several months, and I liked him, but I knew that he was not my true love and I was relieved that he was moving away, because it meant I wouldn't have to suffer through an agonizing conversation about how I didn't want to be his boyfriend. I could just let distance tear us apart.

Knitting scarves and hats and baby blankets had been all well and good, but socks required an entirely different level of commitment. First, the patterns I'd been using for scarves and hats and baby blankets never called for needles smaller than size six; for the socks I needed size one. Second, where for flat garments I had used two needles, socks required four, which complicated things exponentially. And third, Mike had size-eleven feet—it should be clear why I was dating him—and so knitting his socks took *forever*. I walked around Manhattan carrying a set of four long toothpicks, yarn trailing behind me; the bamboo needles were so thin that every other day I'd break one and have to buy a new set. I used self-patterning yarn, however, which is the closest thing this world has to witchcraft: it's dyed in such a way that you don't do a thing but knit it, and the sock you end up with looks like a foot-shaped Rembrandt.

By the time Mike's move was at hand, I had finished only one sock of the pair. In the few days I had left, I tried heroically to complete the other, sitting up nights turning the heel and decreasing like mad, but in the end the task was beyond me. The evening before he was to depart for the frozen north—thank God—I gave him the finished sock and an IOU. I knew I was creating the potential for messiness here: if I'd given him both socks, I could have made a clean break, whereas by incurring a debt I risked maintaining a closer connection to him than I wanted. My plan was therefore to finish the companion sock quickly, send it to him, and then e-dump him.

Unfortunately before I could do so he wrote from Boston asking me what was going on. Were we still boyfriends? Did we have a future? Would I go antiquing with him in the spring? I replied evasively, as was my custom with him. It was not clear to me whether we had ever been boyfriends, I said, I wasn't sure whether we had a future, and I didn't know whether I would go antiquing with him in the spring. All of this was a lie; it was clear, and I was sure, and I did know. But I couldn't bring myself to say so, because he might have gotten mad at me.

He had dated me for nine months, though, and I suspected that he was able to see through this tergiversation to the rejection behind it; my suspicions were strengthened when he didn't respond to my e-mail. This wouldn't have been a problem except for the unfinished sock. The way I saw it, I had three options: 1) I could finish it and send it to him; he was, after all, its intended recipient, and my having broken up with him didn't change that. Or 2) I could finish the sock in my size, get the yarn to make another matching sock, and keep the pair for myself. Or 3) I could leave the sock unfinished, to act as a beacon to my real true love, calling him to me as surely as a siren calls a sailor to the shore. Fate would deposit him on my doorstep, he would tell me his foot size, and I would finish the sock and knit a matching one. In a modern-day Cinderella ending, he would see that the sock fit his foot like . . . well, like a sock, and we would live happily ever after.

I had more or less decided on 3)—if nothing else it would allow me to stop bumping into people as I walked down the street because I was so engrossed in my knitting—when Mike sent me an e-mail with the subject heading "I want my sock!" It was an extraordinary piece of writing, full of forgiveness and warmth and wit. If I had been a character in a novel, this would have made me fall in love with him and we would have ended up getting married. Sadly, I was not a character in a novel. I moped around my apartment for the rest of the day, knowing that no one would ever love me and that I didn't deserve to be loved anyway. Then I had sex with a stranger and on the 1 train back from his apartment I finished the sock, which I sent Mike the next day along with a lame note.

As I stood in line at the post office, sock-filled envelope in hand, I looked up at the grubby calendar on the wall and realized that it was ten years almost to the day I had last seen my mother alive. By the time I finished high school, the two of us had reached a détente: she no longer voiced any displeasure with my choice to be openly gay, and I did not push her for more. But the rift between us never mended completely. In 1992, in the morning hours before I left for my sophomore year of college, we sat together on the porch of my family's ramshackle beach house and watched the tide ebb out to sea, knowing she would not live to see Thanksgiving. From the stereo inside, Joan Baez sang a song about the honest lullaby her mother had sung her, a song my mother had taught me years before, guitar on her knee and tenderness in her voice.

"We've had a lot of time together," my mother said to me as the waves washed farther and farther away, "and a lot of that time we've been really close, so it's as if we'd had twice as much time as we've actually had." As we laughed the next song started, about how for all we knew we might never meet again, and we had to love each other tonight because tomorrow might never come.

My father came out to tell me we had to leave for the airport. I stayed put, because I knew what was coming next; moments later the air vibrated with Joan's rendition of the spiritual from which thousands of people had drawn strength for hundreds of years. She was free at last, she sang, free from the world and all its sin; she was free at last, for she had been to the top of the mountain.

"Goodbye, Mom," I said, and walked out to the idling car.

A few months later, the day before the 1992 presidential election, my father called to tell me my mother wasn't long for this world. I flew home that night, but she, lying on a knitted blanket in her pale, wasted frame and her clean blue-and-white nightgown, barely breathing, had really already left, and nothing I could say would matter to her now. I flew back north the next morning. Her final earthly act of *tikkun olam* had been to sign her absentee ballot; shortly after Bill Clinton's victory speech, she breathed her last. After my father called to give me the news, at two or three in the morning, I went to the campus church—I helped run the choir, so I had keys—and sat for an hour at the organ playing my favorite hymn: *Deck thyself, my soul, with gladness! Leave the gloomy haunts of sadness; come into the daylight's splendor!* Then I called my friend Peter and we went out for pizza and he obviously wanted to console me but I did not meet his gaze and when we spoke it was only to gossip about friends and professors because what I felt was unnameable and because I feared putting it into words would shatter me.

Yesterday, after finishing a pair of socks for my friend Victoria, I started knitting a polka-dotted tea cozy. This is my first felted project; that is to say, once I'm finished knitting it, I'll put it in the washing machine and when I take it out it will be not a shapeless mass full of little holes but a piece of imperforate green, lavender, orange, and light blue polka-dotted felt the perfect shape and size to keep a teapot warm.

The pattern I'm using requires only a small amount of the light blue yarn, but almost right away I found myself working it into places it wasn't called for. The blue is the exact color of my mother's dress in the painting that hung above my family's fireplace for years; the oils depicted a four-year-old with short hair and a little ball in her hands. I asked her once why she looked so sad in the painting. "I was terrified," she said. "Your grandmother wanted me holding that ball in the painting but I almost hadn't been able to find it. And I knew what would happen if I made her angry."

"Why is the painting up there if it's such an unhappy memory?"

"So I can look at it every day and remind myself that I vowed never to do to my children what my mother did to me."

And I believe my mother kept that vow.

So how then can she have done everything within her power to protect me and yet still not have done enough? How is it that into the boundless love I feel for her is woven inextricably such a boundless rage? How, if there is a merciful Mother, am I not remade and restored?

Last night I didn't get much sleep, because, as usually happens when I begin a new knitting project, I stayed awake long past my bedtime, turning the lights off and saying to myself again and again that I would knit (or purl) just one more round and then I would go to sleep. There was a *Law & Order: SVU* marathon on and for a while I concentrated on Chris Meloni as I worked, but when I turned the TV off there was still light coming in through my window from the streetlamp outside, so I continued to knit in silence and watched the fabric growing in my hands.

On Casual Sex

*I*t was sometime in the fall of 2001, I believe, that Tom broke up with me. It may very well have been on Thursday, October 17, at 8:12 in the evening, in an anticlimactic conversation on Broadway between Eighty-fifth and Eighty-sixth, on the east side of the street, just north of French Roast—but really, who can remember these things after so much time has passed?

We were one of several Manhattan couples I knew whose relationships didn't survive the terrorist attacks on September 11, but I suspect that the writing had been on the wall for us well before the planes flew into the World Trade Center. That night, as I sat stunned in front of the television, staring at Paula Zahn with glassy eyes, Tom stepped over to me and put a hand on my shoulder and said gently, "We'll come through this. There will always be evil in the world, but you'll see—America will be courageous enough to face this and in the end we'll only become a stronger nation."

And I looked up at him and, through my tears, I found the strength somewhere to shriek, "Who gives a *fuck* about that when *YOU FORGOT TO TAKE THE DOG OUT LAST NIGHT?*"

We started seeing a couples therapist, hoping to repair whatever fraying bond still connected us, but he told us in the middle of our third session that we really needed to break up. So we took his advice, and then I did what any sensible gay man of ~~twenty-nine~~ ~~twenty-eight~~ twenty-six in my position would do: I became a ravening slut.

As I see it, the problem with heterosexual sex is that it involves two creatures whose evolution (if biologists are to be believed) has given them conflicting needs. For women, I am given to understand, physical desire and emotional intimacy go hand in hand. Men are not like this. We just want sex. And since the people gay men want sex with, being men themselves, *also* just want sex, everything becomes remarkably easy, at least for those who wish it to be. Many don't wish it to be, of course, and of course even the most promiscuous among us can also dream of a lasting connection to a man with whom to raise children or at least a small dog. But casual sex tends to be a much simpler proposition. The individuals involved don't run into each other again, at least not until we're at a party with a date and realize we have to avoid five-eighths of the men in the room because we can't remember their names.

I had never been a slut before. Tom had been my first real boyfriend, but even prior to meeting him I had not held the idea of casual sex in high esteem. When I came out of the closet in junior high, my head was filled with fantasies of a man who would bring me flowers and—would God I were making this up—take me for walks on the beach. Never mind that I cry when I get sand in my shoes; I still wanted to date a Hallmark card. By the time I finished college, I had gotten over my naive insistence that sex and love were inextricably intertwined. I was still foolish enough, however, to believe that intercourse was somehow more magical if you had seen your partner in more than one shirt.

Then I moved to New York.

Ah, New York, the cradle of Gay Liberation, where you can so comport yourself as to be incapable of walking a block without bumping into somebody you've slept with. Yet for a long time the night found me far more often in the arms of Morpheus than of, um, Whatshisname. This was partially because I was throwing all my energy into my graduate program in musical theater writing; mostly, though, it was because I was fat. Compared with much of the rest of America, I was average, or perhaps slightly overweight; furthermore, I am shaped in such a way that I didn't look as big as I could have. But in gay weight I was Jabba the Hutt. During the holidays I was Jabba the Hutt's fatter cousin, the one who goes to Hutt family barbecues and is offered celery sticks.

But my weight plummeted in the waning days of my relationship, as I found myself doing things like consuming the entirety of an Entenmann's Chocolate Fudge Cake for breakfast and then eating nothing else until the next morning. Occasionally, in the days immediately following Tom's departure, I would open the kitchen cabinet and catch sight of, say, a package of Kraft Macaroni and Cheese, and instead of eating it I would dissolve into impassioned sobs when I recalled that *Tom and I had once eaten Kraft Macaroni and Cheese together.*

Gradually, however, pasta lost the power to make me want to kill myself, and one morning I realized that, far from rendering me unlovable, being svelte, single, and ~~twenty-six~~ twenty-five opened up a world of possibility to me. I was free—free to spread my fledgling wings, free to become the person I wanted to be, free to soar in search of my soul. So I joined men4sexnow.com.

Thank God somebody invented the Internet. I have trouble ordering pizza because I'm scared I'll make a mistake and the guy on the other end of the phone will immediately realize that I am so far beneath his notice I'm not even worth mocking. Naturally, then, the idea of going to a bar and trying to figure out whether the look a cute guy was giving me meant "let's go back to my place and have the kind of sex we'll both remember for the rest of our days" or "oh, yuck" made me want to peel my skin off. My fragile psyche was simply not up to the task.

Men4sexnow.com was therefore a greater boon to me than I suspect its architects imagined, as the system is designed to eliminate even the slightest trace of uncertainty. Anybody who has spent time on a dating website will be familiar with the principles of online matches; the only difference on men4sexnow.com is that no one pretends to care who your favorite authors are. Instead, you list information of actual practical value—the measurements of relevant body parts, the times of day you're available for liaisons, and, most importantly, your sexual interests ("Jacking Off," "Spanking," "Anything Goes"). The parameters of the database to which you are then allowed access are marvelously specific: you can look for Latino bottoms who are HIV-positive and willing to "host" (as opposed to "traveling"); you can look for tops under the age of twenty-three who live in your borough and are over six feet tall; you can look for men who feel a sense of existential despair so crushing as nearly to prevent them from leaving their apartments in the morning and who are uncircumcised and into public sex.

With such a comprehensive search apparatus at my disposal, it was not long before I made my first contact. Browsing the list of members one Friday night (I hadn't yet sunk to trolling for anonymous sex on Tuesday morning, though I would reach such a pass soon enough), I saw a picture of an attractive man with salt-and-pepper hair whose carnal interests matched mine ("1 on 1 Sex"). The sticking point was that I lived in Washington Heights and he lived in the Financial District, which, for the benefit of those who have never been to Manhattan, is like saying I lived in Montreal and he lived in Buenos Aires. But as a budding harlot I realized I would never reach full bloom without making a few sacrifices, so I agreed to meet him at his apartment.

On the A train downtown I flipped through a copy of *Us Weekly*, pausing here and there to read more about Rupert Everett's hair or the Olsen twins' deep appreciation of vinyasa yoga. Then I saw an item about Johnny Depp and a movie in which he was going to be playing *Peter Pan* author J. M. Barrie, and I was transfixed.

I have worshipped Johnny Depp ever since the premiere, when I was fourteen, of *21 Jump Street*, the television series that launched the Fox network and rocketed him to stardom. I looked forward to the first episode as if it were Christmas without the drunk relatives. Cops going secretly into high schools where they would doubtless make drug busts in locker rooms filled with half-naked football players still dirty from the field or wet from the shower—what could possibly be more appealing to a boy feeling the first stirrings of something to which he couldn't even put a name? Or, rather, of something to which he could put a name but the name was *sissy homo faggot*?

In the *21 Jump Street* pilot, Johnny Depp played the strait-laced Officer Tom Hanson, transferred unwillingly to the Jump Street Unit. This was a band of ephebic police officers who, under the guidance of the tatterdemalion Captain Jenko, disguised themselves as Cool Kids and infiltrated schools at which there were Problems. Upon Hanson's arrival, the other officers took one look at his starched shirt and barbershop haircut and realized there was no way he could pass for a Cool Kid without a major overhaul. And so in a two-minute montage accompanied by Steve Winwood's "Back in the High Life Again," Officer Huffs (played by the incomprehensibly beautiful Holly Robinson) turned him into a completely different person. She outfitted him in stonewashed jeans and a leather jacket; she teased his hair to an altitude I found dangerously seductive (this was, after all, 1987); she took him to an arcade where she taught him to play video games, eat hot dogs, and laugh, three activities in which he had apparently never before engaged; she corrected his taste in LPs by discarding his choices at the record store in favor of other, more stylish albums; and, finally, she pierced his left ear—in those days only fags pierced their right ears—and adorned it with an earring the size of a chandelier. To top it all off, a stern but supportive Captain Jenko educated him on the Cool Kids' two basic food groups, potato chips and soda. "Back in the High Life Again" faded out and there stood sneering disciplinary nightmare Tom Bauer, dripping disdain on the outside but secretly ready to come to the rescue of any troubled high school student who needed him.

The episode went on for another hour and a half but those two minutes had imprinted themselves so spectacularly on my brain that I paid very little attention.

It wasn't that I was in love with Johnny Depp. Of course I *was* in love with Johnny Depp, but my fascination ran deeper than that. I had spent my life being overjoyed to do as I was expected to do—overjoyed to get good grades, overjoyed to be polite, overjoyed to speak when spoken to—because I had no idea that the universe admitted of any other choice. Before *21 Jump Street* I had never seen anybody break the mold in which society had cast him and assume instead a shape of his own choosing. I had never before seen somebody I admired understand what was expected of him, choose to act otherwise, and be happier for it. For the first time in my life I realized that it was possible to reinvent oneself.

So I reinvented my adolescent self, with a vengeance, in the image of Johnny Depp.

All right, not *exactly* in the image of Johnny Depp. He had dark hair and cheekbones with which one could slit one's wrists; I was a redhead and my acne was so bad it eventually required pharmacological intervention. He was a heroic TV star; I was a fey child secretly delighted by the rumors that I had read the *Encyclopædia Britannica* for fun. Nevertheless, I had grasped the essence of Johnny Depp's makeover, and I swung into action. I bought some corduroy pants and a pair of Jams from JCPenney to supplement the school-approved khaki slacks of which most of my wardrobe had until now been composed. I bought a week's supply of Snickers bars to eat for breakfast and gum to chew at school (though only during break and lunch, since chewing gum during class was against the rules). I looked in the Yellow Pages under "Hair" for the trendiest-sounding establishment I could find, which proved to be a place called Whispers Hair in Motion. Puzzled briefly by the absence of a subject—"*Who* whispers hair in motion?" I kept asking myself; "*Who? Who?*"—I decided that, mystifying syntax notwithstanding, this would still be a vast improvement over Mooney's Barber Shop. When I arrived for my appointment at what I had come to think of as Whispers: Hair in Motion, my stylist introduced himself as Jean. At the time he seemed both ancient and French, but the wisdom that has come with age tells me he was thirty-two and faking the accent. I was both tantalized and deeply disturbed when he flirtatiously aimed the blow-dryer at my crotch after giving me a haircut that, in South Carolina in the days when people still knew who Soleil Moon Frye was, might as well have come straight off the runway in Milan.

Of course the corduroy pants went in the wash at some point, and Jams were against the school dress code, so I had to wear the khakis again, and after I spent all my allowance on Snickers I had to go back to Rice Krispies for breakfast, and when break and lunch arrived I usually forgot to chew gum. I did continue to patronize Whispers: Hair in Motion for a few years, but I was never brave enough to take Jean up on his offer of a massage at his apartment. Eventually he gave me far too stylish a haircut the day before my junior prom, and I dumped him for TJ of TJ's Hair Space.

But what remained through college and into what passed for my adulthood was the delectable, slightly unsettling knowledge that I could decide for myself who I wanted to be, and that I could make that decision as easily as I could, alas, put on a pair of Jams. This had been my governing principle since the premiere of *21 Jump Street,* even though the show went off the air in 1991. The summer I decided to become a strictly observant Jew; the year I spent at the gym making myself buff; the semester I started wearing vests and a pocket watch—it was Johnny Depp who had made them all possible. Officers Hanson, Huff, Ioki, and Penhall were eventually supplanted on Fox by the ravings of Ann Coulter, but I kept reforging myself over and over in the fires of whatever fancies seized me.

And eventually those fancies had brought me here, to the downtown subway headed toward the Financial District for sex, wondering where this new path in life would lead. Would I emerge from the Whitehall Street station into the world of glamour and glitz and laughter I had heretofore only glimpsed from afar through the pages of *XY Magazine*? Would I become the apparently jaded but secretly wise and joyful roué I had dreamed of being for so long? Or were these images merely myths created by the gay media working in concert with my own potent self-doubt? But I realized as I switched to the R train at Forty-second Street that there was no way to divine the answer. In fact, I thought as I knocked on a door I'd never seen before, wasn't that the point of this whole exercise? To leap without looking?

So of course I totally knew him and we spent like half an hour gossiping about musical theater before we did anything else.

Okay, I didn't *know* him, technically speaking, but I knew who he was (a prominent Broadway choreographer) and he knew who I was (a non-prominent non-Broadway composer). In person he fulfilled the promise of sexiness hinted at in his online photograph, and after we finished trading rumors about which shows were in trouble out of town a silence filled the room. Over the course of our conversation we'd maneuvered ourselves closer together on the couch; now he drew my head gently nearer to his, opened his lips sensually—oh, so sensually—and rammed his tongue into my mouth as if he were trying to bring down the gates of Masada.

The situation did not improve from there. I considered calling the whole thing off, but he seemed so enthusiastic I felt it would be churlish of me to leave. The only way to get him to stop Hoovering my mouth seemed therefore to be to start the 1 on 1 Sex as quickly as possible; I feigned such eagerness for this to happen as to be unable to restrain myself. Don't get me wrong—I *was* eager. After all, there was always the chance that foreplay simply wasn't his métier, and that what he lacked here he would more than make up for once we really got going. And so, without breaking the kiss (how could I, when the vacuum seal he'd created between our mouths was so strong as to be invulnerable to nuclear fission?), I took my jeans off.

"What, no underwear?" he chuckled. "My, my, aren't we excited?"

"No," I wanted to say, "the washing machines in our building are broken and so we're out of clean boxer briefs and on rent strike," but I was so relieved to be able once more to draw breath that I couldn't get the words out. He leaned in to kiss me again; to avoid this, I executed a horizontal triple lutz at a velocity Michelle Kwan would have envied, and landed prone among the tasteful pillows. He responded by lifting me up chivalrously and carrying me—I am pleased to note here that I was light enough to cause no unseemly grunting on his part—into the bedroom, where he subjected me to the most tedious twenty minutes I had experienced since I could remember.

This is not to say that I derived no pleasure from our congress; certainly I felt the physical gratification that usually attends the activity in which we were engaged. But still, between occasional winces of discomfort, I wondered: Where was the subtlety? Where was the *ritardando,* the *crescendo,* the *subito piano?* Where was the lube?

Finally, after I had composed the B section to the song I was working on and remembered where I'd left my copy of *Miss Manners' Guide to Excruciatingly Correct Behavior,* he started screwing his face up, letting his tongue loll out of his mouth, and grunting incomprehensibly. I delightedly understood this to be the universal sign for "I'm coming!" and released the psychic and physical restraint in which I'd been holding myself. I screwed up my face and lolled and grunted right along with him, because I didn't want him to think I wasn't having a good time, and we were done, if not exactly at the same moment— the Holy Grail of casual sex—then close enough at least to feel that we'd made a good show of it.

We lay on our backs, breathing deeply, and I basked in the feeling of being connected, however haphazardly and for however brief a time, to another human soul. After a quarter of an hour I got out of bed and pulled my clothes on. A quick kiss goodbye and a vague "See you around" and I was gone.

I waited a long time for the subway back home. How had this happened? For years I'd heard gays described in the most salacious terms as fornicators hungry for nothing but spiritually empty sins of the flesh. How then could the practice of those sins have turned out to be such a workaday event? Where was the glamour and glitz and laughter? Why wasn't I now a jaded but secretly wise and joyful roué?

And why, most of all, was there a bounce in my step? I felt just as unfulfilled as I had two hours before. Shouldn't I have been moping about not having gotten what I wanted?

And then it occurred to me that perhaps I had gotten something else instead.

The first gay book I ever bought, in the summer after eighth grade, was a slim volume called *I'm looking for Mr. Right but I'll settle for Mr. Right Away*. I found it in a New Age bookstore in Los Angeles called the Bodhi Tree, and in order to camouflage my purchase I also bought copies of *The Journeyman's Tarot* and *Your Inner Child of the Past*. The clerk saw through my ruse, however, and yelled at the top of his lungs, "I'M LOOKING FOR MR. RIGHT BUT I'LL SETTLE

FOR MR. RIGHT AWAY—NOPE, NO SIR, THAT'S NOT THE WAY TO GO, YOU HAVE TO WAIT FOR MR. RIGHT!" None of the other customers batted a dharma-laden eyelash, but I hurled my cash on the counter and fled as if the Nazis were coming. Eventually, having reached a safe distance from the store and from any human population, I began to read. The thrust of *I'm looking for Mr. Right but I'll settle for Mr. Right Away* was that fleeting, anonymous sex filled no spiritual or emotional void at all.

And I was like, well, *duh.*

But, as I reflected on the subway back uptown, spiritual and emotional fulfillment weren't what I had been after here. It wasn't as if I had thought casual sex with somebody I had never met would fill the gaping chasms that two and a half years of a bad relationship had gouged irreparably into my spirit, or give me the sense of deep intimacy I had not felt since *The Golden Girls* ended its run. No, I had just wanted to reinvent myself again, but with sex instead of Snickers. I had wanted to break the mold in which my boyfriend had cast me and to assume instead a shape of my own choosing.

And to that end I had embraced the risks and wonders offered by the anonymity of a casual encounter. I had put all my faith in myself and in my own potential, I had celebrated the holiness of my sexuality. True, I had spent much of the previous hour with somebody who had lifted half his last show's choreography from Michael Jackson videos; still, I had been bold enough to go in search of that somebody, to whose name I would never have given a face but for an accident of fate, and ask him to skewer me.

Back in the high life, indeed.

My career as a slut, so auspiciously begun, progressed apace. Some of the men I met were just as maladroit in bed as the choreographer; some were worse. A few were more technically accomplished, but handicapped themselves in other ways. Take, for example, the Scottish gentleman who, when not rutting with strangers, worked as a professional masseur. I arrived at his apartment one Sunday afternoon and was thrilled when he invited me onto his massage table and started oiling my body; clearly I was going to get sex *and* a back rub. But, sadly, it wasn't to be. He stopped the massage far too early and soon enough he was plunging in and out of me, which was quite pleasant until he started grunting about how he loved to fuck my pussy. He used the word "pussy" forty-seven times. When we were done I went home and e-mailed the Scottish embassy in New York suggesting that they revamp their human anatomy curricula, but they never wrote back.

Then there was the fellow whose (straight) wedding ring so scandalized me that I almost ripped his pants taking them off. His marriage to a woman notwithstanding, he was either an experienced sodomite or a natural genius. At some point during coitus, however, he switched from calling me "Peter Pan," which I liked (especially after a brief fantasy of Johnny Depp as J. M. Barrie walking in and joining us), to calling me "little whore," which I didn't. But how to object? Any remonstrance would completely destroy the tone of the encounter, which was otherwise most agreeable. And I couldn't meaningfully refuse him access to my inmost depths, as there was no part of my inmost depths he hadn't already accessed. Then circumstances provided me with the perfect opportunity to defend my honor, and my mother wit was for once quick enough to take immediate advantage of it. And so, for the first time in my life, I spat instead of swallowing.

A week later I e-mailed him asking whether he'd be interested in meeting again—disagreeable epithets aside, he had been a master of his craft—and he replied that he would. In my response to him I mentioned that I'd dyed my hair black, and I never heard from him again; if I was no longer a redhead, I suppose, he couldn't imagine that he was fucking the Boy Who Wouldn't Grow Up.

There were also the occasional (the *very* occasional) meetings that I found enjoyable on almost every level. There was Dan, for example, possessed of an extraordinary body and, it seemed, a personality to match. I arrived at his apartment to find not only that it was bursting with greenery but also that there was a dog-eared copy of *Persuasion* on the coffee table. Dan was great in bed, tender and rough by turns; all the plants made the sex feel that much more alive, and the Austen made me feel, as she always does, that there was still hope for civilization. Dan and I met once more and then he ruined everything by acquiring a boyfriend.

But Dan was the exception rather than the rule. In the few moments each day that I wasn't on my back mentally translating Top 40 hits from my childhood into French ("Only the Good Die Young" proved particularly insusceptible of idiomatic felicity), I wondered. Yes, my continual auto-reinvention was in essence a solitary activity, so it didn't really matter whether my partners had awkward technique or discomfiting pillow talk or, in one frightening instance, a pet python. But still, how was it that the sex was so consistently wretched?

And then it occurred to me that, if I was re-creating myself, maybe my partners were too. The waiter who slathered vile-tasting moisturizer all over his body five minutes before I showed up, the Streisand enthusiast who wouldn't shut up about organic produce, the bodybuilder whose user name was jimjones (I actually couldn't bring myself to go through with that one, especially as I had a weird feeling when I read his e-mail and I checked the date and it was the twenty-fifth anniversary of the Jonestown massacre, so he may very well have been a sexual dynamo, but I'll never know)—maybe they had joined men4sexnow.com for the same reasons I had: they were weary of who they had allowed themselves to become, and were making themselves over by boffing strangers. And if this was so then I was giving them as much as they were giving me.

My pride swelled from liaison to liaison. Sure, I may have just had sex with a guy who wore a spiked collar and spanked me with something made out of leather and then pulled off the blindfold he'd insisted I wear only to reveal a room filled with *Star Wars* figures, Luke Skywalker in a different outfit everywhere I looked—but hadn't I also just become a person who could dare to do such things? Wasn't I exploring farther reaches of this new territory every day, erasing boundaries with every drop of my trousers? Wasn't my character becoming measureless? And wasn't his, too? Weren't we both complicit in the collective expansion of the human soul?

Inevitably this led to orgies.

Repeated viewings of *Gang Bang Cadet* and *The Dicks of Hazzard* had convinced me that to participate in group sex was to reach the zenith of fleshly delights. The writhing mass of groaning, grunting, grasping carnality on my television screen promised a bacchanalian unity of spirit not otherwise seen outside of a Kylie Minogue concert. Come on, I thought: twelve or so well-proportioned (or so the hosts vowed) men

reveling in one another's bodies, laughing at the antiquated in-
hibitions we had discarded at the door along with our clothing.
What could possibly keep such an event from being epiphanic?

The answer, of course, is elbows. What *Gang Bang Cadet*
and *The Dicks of Hazzard* fail to disclose is that group sex is
among the most physically uncomfortable businesses in which
it is possible for a human being to engage. At one point during
my first orgy I found myself lying diagonally across a bed, tenuously attached to somebody whose technique was hampered
by his being tenuously attached in turn to somebody else; he
kept going too far in one direction or the other and accidentally detaching himself from one or the other of us. The fellow
on my right was reaching for the fellow on his right, who was
unfortunately too far away for him to get to without removing
his tongue from where it was already delighting a third fellow
I couldn't see.

And the awkwardness wasn't confined to the realm of the
physical. One pudgy guy kept leaning over as if to do something to me with his mouth but hesitating; I couldn't reassure
him, since I didn't know what he was scared of. Across the
crowded room was a bleach blond with whom I kept making
the kind of electrical eye contact that portended great sex, but
during the entire evening we never had the matching body
parts free at the same time. All of us were starting to reek, because we'd followed protocol and not worn deodorant, in case
somebody wanted to lick our armpits, and all of us were
clenching our abs the whole time for fear that somebody might
notice halfway through that we were fat.

But here was a unity of spirit all the same; it was simply
collegial rather than bacchanalian. We all had our reasons for
coming here, after all, self-transformational or otherwise, and
we were all more than happy to help one another achieve our

respective goals. The pudgy guy eventually did—very effectively—the thing he'd been working up the courage to do. I never did connect with the blond across the room, but the only thing that meant was that when the gathering ended I could leave trusting I hadn't exhausted whatever promise the night held. This trust was borne out when on the subway home I started knitting what turned out to be a really great hat.

After mastering orgies I thought it only natural to expand my repertoire to include sex clubs. These are venues at which one pays a modest entrance fee and takes one's chances with the other patrons. A sex club is like an orgy to which everybody is invited—democracy taken to its logical extreme, the elitist monarchy overthrown in favor of the all-embracing Republic. Louis XVI would have an orgy; Robespierre would go to a sex club, though not, I hope, on a night I was there.

There are two differences between an orgy and a sex club. First, at a sex club it's considered bad form to introduce yourself to someone before you start putting parts of his body in your mouth. At an orgy you are allowed to offer your name as long as you do so with an obvious sense of irony.

The second difference between an orgy and a sex club is that at a sex club the snacks are wrapped hard candies, while at an orgy they are cold cuts, or, if the hosts are really classy, canapés.

During the period of Dionysiac frenzy I had entered I did not abandon the more intimate tête-à-têtes with which I had begun my journey, though these continued to be of a woefully inconsistent quality. There was the man with the fabulous apartment in the West Village who told me after we were done that I wasn't enough of a top for him, a complaint that would have held more validity if the heading on my men4sexnow.com profile hadn't read "Tight Bottom." Then there was the man in the eerily familiar apartment; I realized halfway through our assignation that it was familiar because I had gone on an actual *date* date with its previous occupant disastrous enough to leave me in tears for hours (we made out for ten minutes and then he said, "Um, I'm not really into this" and kicked me out). The sex the second time around wasn't particularly memorable but I felt I had conquered the genius of the place, and I left whistling. There was Biff, who made me call him Sir and whose harsh "I didn't *tell* you to suck it" sent thrills down my spine surpassed only by the thrills sent down my spine by what he did when I did what he *had* told me to do.

But at some point I noticed with surprise that my energy had begun to flag, my enthusiasm to wane. I found myself inviting men to my apartment—something I had almost never done before, in case of serial killers—because I couldn't bear the thought of the subway ride. There was Vlad, for example, who smelled bad but whom I slept with anyway simply so as to be able to make jokes to my friends about Vlad the Impaler. He left my apartment and instead of the joy I had learned to take in reshaping my character I found myself just feeling annoyed. Well, annoyed and smelly, but while a shower took care of the latter it left the former untouched. There were the orgy hosts who proved to be a hard-lived ten years older than they appeared in the photo they had sent me. I didn't know how to excuse myself gracefully, so I threw myself into the festivities with as much gusto as I could manage. My discomfort increased considerably when I realized that the only other participants were going to be a man with a disfiguring birthmark and another man who kept up a running monologue about his wife, but by this time it was too late for me to leave, as I had already committed myself at both ends. And I spent the whole time wondering whether I was on row five or seven of my sweater pattern, and wanting ice cream, and wishing I were reading *Pride and Prejudice*. Not that this encounter was so materially different from earlier ones like it; but somehow I went home feeling not invigorated but exhausted.

And then I actually started *turning down* sex. He lived too far away, I told myself, or it was late and I had to get up early the next day. Or it was early and I didn't want to deal with the rush-hour crowd. Or I was tired.

Tired? I asked myself. Tired of traversing a self I hadn't even known existed? Tired of searching for the unknown and, once I had found it, letting it sit on my face?

What was happening? Was my soul, until recently so expansive, shriveling and calcifying by the day? Was I losing the capacity to remake myself?

Was I getting old?

And then I stopped. I wish I could say it happened dramatically, one fateful day, but it was more a gentle dwindling. I canceled my subscription to men4sexnow.com. I stopped answering e-mails from men who had enjoyed the pleasure of my company and who wished to do so again. I stopped going to orgies and sex clubs. I went back into the low life.

And I ached with loss—but loss of what, I didn't know. I fought it by filling my time with productive activity. I wrote more, I composed more, I worked more. At first such pursuits didn't ease the ache at all but gradually, over the three or four years that have passed since then, it has subsided to the point at which I don't notice it anymore.

Mostly.

Last week, though, my computer informed me that its

memory banks were almost full and that, in order to avoid risking the integrity of my hard drive, I ought to divest myself of all unnecessary data. A cursory inventory of the largest files revealed several video clips the deletion of which would have been foolish given the frequency with which my boyfriend is on overnight call at the hospital, so I went in search of other potential jetsam.

Further exploration led me to a number of folders the contents of which I hadn't examined for years. Among the masterfully snide letters of complaint and the drafts of college papers I'd kept because they reminded me of the TA with the cute ass I came upon a file called ship.jpg and was suddenly overcome with nostalgia.

During my gradual adieu to the fleshpots, I had deleted most of the pictures men had e-mailed me along with offers to have their way with me; since very few of these images showed their subjects' faces they had been more or less indistinguishable anyway, with a few impressive exceptions. But ship.jpg, along with a handful of other photographs, had escaped its fellows' fate. Though I hadn't looked at the picture for years I did not have to open the file to remember it well: It depicted a young Latino man standing in some sort of festive gathering area, his hands grasping the lattice of the low ceiling above him, a wide enough gap on his left side between the hem of his shirt and the waist of his pants to reveal a small but tantalizing expanse of smooth skin stretched taut over cut muscle. The viewer had but a moment to consider this feature, however, before being practically blinded by the stunning face above it, upon which was fixed a smile of utter sweetness that yet managed to convey a sense of depravity the depths of which one is lucky to dream of encountering. I was not so naive as to pine for this gentleman as the One That Got Away, but I had spent an occasional moment or three over the years wishing that he and I might have enjoyed an afternoon together, or at least a lunch hour.

As I double-clicked on the file I felt a frisson of regret at the thought of all the potential in the world. There are men to be had, I thought, men who will pull me into their arms and their apartments and spear me without knowing my name or, possibly, how to spell; but I have lost the knack for reshaping myself, and they are beyond my reach.

I sat back in my chair as the file opened and prepared for the fond reminiscence of a time long gone. The man whose memory had given me so many pleasant moments appeared on my screen.

And he was totally plain.

He had mediocre teeth, and, though the photographer had caught his face at a good angle, two seconds of further examination revealed a visage no more comely than average, and from certain angles less so.

The units did not exist capable of measuring my disappointment. How could ship.jpg have betrayed me so? Or was it my critical faculties that had betrayed me by changing their standards as I aged? The frisson of regret I had felt before opening the file was slipping away moment by moment, but I could not help suspecting that it was taking with it my sense of possibility.

I deleted the file, put my computer to sleep, and left my desk. On the way upstairs I caught sight of myself in the hallway mirror and realized that, no matter what shape I took, the raw material would remain the same and that, no matter who I imagine myself to be, my reflection will never show me anyone better than I am.

I knew I had to take strong measures to keep from sinking further toward despair, so I hurried to the bookcase for some Austen. After a few seconds' thought, I settled on *Sense and Sensibility*, but though I searched the shelves for twenty minutes, *I'm looking for Mr. Right but I'll settle for Mr. Right Away* was all I could find.

On Cheerleading

"*L*et's watch ESPN," said my brother, grabbing the remote control. It was Thanksgiving morning, and we were lolling around the apartment we shared, whiling away the hours before dinner with my friend Debbie. We had no interest in watching the repulsive Macy's Thanksgiving Day Parade. I had lobbied for *The Christopher Lowell Show,* a program in which a flaming homosexual redecorates houses using only Elmer's Glue and staples, but Jeremy would have none of it.

As the TV flickered on, I opened my mouth to start complaining so insufferably that he would be forced to change the channel, but before I could speak I was silenced by what I saw on the screen in front of me. It was a college cheerleading championship. Thirty fresh-faced cheerleaders, boys and girls, were running around in perky uniforms, grinning like madpeople, shouting cheers as they flipped their way across a mat and threw one another thirty feet in the air and caught one another on the way down. It was like *Bring It On,* only real.

I was instantly filled with self-loathing. During the activities fair in the first week of college, years before, I had stopped at the cheerleading table, but by the time they called to let me know about the informational meeting I had already scheduled a conflicting choir audition, so I decided not to become a cheerleader. (I also decided not to become a fencer or an appreciator of modern dance, and though I did go to a meeting of the Theosophical Society because I had a crush on one of its members, in the end the fact that nothing anybody said there made any sense proved stronger than my attraction to Jason's cheekbones, and I didn't go back.) But now, watching these children, practically children, flying into the air as if adulthood weren't waiting on the ground to pounce once they came down, I was overwhelmed with regret that I had squandered my youth in serious pursuits. Choir, indeed. I should have been a cheerleader, and now it was just too fucking late.

But after half an hour or so of vicious self-excoriation, I stopped short. *Wait a second,* I thought. *I'm a twentysomething gay man living in Manhattan. There's **got** to be a cheerleading squad I can join.*

And, as if it had read my mind, Google took me posthaste to the website for Cheer New York. More alive with joy than I had been since seeing my first opera at age six (*The Marriage of Figaro*), I left a giddy voice mail saying I was interested in joining the squad; on the way to dinner I made Debbie hold my keys and wallet and change while I executed a front handspring, the most complicated move I remembered from the gymnastics I'd done at Jewish Community Center summer camp when I was six. I landed precariously—I'd forgotten most of what they taught me in camp about equilibrium—but in the end I kept my balance. "I'm going to be a cheerleader!" I said, and when we got to the restaurant I was so inspired by my new life as a cheerleader-elect that I almost ordered a salad for Thanksgiving dinner. Then I saw the pie the waiter was bringing to somebody else's table and I figured I could just as easily start my life as a cheerleader-elect the next day. During our meal I could barely concentrate on the conversation, so enthralled was I by fantasies of doing flips and getting thrown in the air and being caught on the way down by a fellow cheerleader who would fall in love with me and get me a dog named Spiffy and make me happy forever.

Unfortunately, when I visited the Cheer New York website again after dinner, I realized that joining the squad wasn't going to be quite as easy as I'd expected, because, according to the bios on the "About Us" page, every single member was either a gymnast, a professional dancer, or a former college cheerleader. The rudimentary front handspring I had performed for Debbie and my brother on the sidewalk was the most difficult gymnastic feat of which I was capable. I had taken some dance classes the summer after I finished college, from a woman named LaToya who kept a studio behind her hair salon. I would show up on Tuesdays and Thursdays at noon and spend an hour and a half attempting to plié and pas de chat and pirouette. The only other student in the class was twelve, and she was better than me. After class one day I asked LaToya if I could get a haircut; I may have been the first white person whose hair she had ever styled, but she did an excellent job. After brushing the stray hairs off my neck, she told me she was putting the dance classes on hold for the rest of the summer. I suspect she simply didn't have the heart to tell me that I was not cut out for a life of kicks and chaînés.

And so now it was with a heavy heart that I shut my computer down, made three cups of chocolate pudding, and turned on the *Golden Girls* marathon on Lifetime Television for Women and Gay Men. I would obviously never make the cheerleading squad. I was barely able to brush my teeth without tripping; what could I hope to contribute to a cheerleading squad populated by experts? I finished the pudding and considered making more. The best dream I had ever had was dead, and in its place I felt a void that not even the Golden Girls' biting insouciance could fill, not even in the episode where they sneak into somebody else's high school reunion so they can meet men and Rose has to pretend to be the school's Korean exchange student Kim Fung-Toy.

But the next morning, when I went again to the Cheer New York website immediately upon waking up not that I was obsessed or anything, I understood that fate had spoken, because there was a new section that said they were having try outs in a week and a half. If I had to claim to be a gymnast or a professional dancer or a former college cheerleader in order to make it onto the squad, then so be it; neither mortal nor god was going to keep me away from the Alfred E. Smith Recreation Center come Monday week.

When the appointed day arrived and I walked into the huge gym on the second floor of the dilapidated building, it appeared empty at first, but then through an open door at the back I saw a group of homosexuals filling out pieces of paper en masse. I joined them and started answering the questions on the form they gave me. Mercifully, it did not ask anything about dancing or gymnastics or prior cheerleading experience. There was a section for "Special Skills" in which I wrote "speak French, German, Italian proficiently; have eliminated gag reflex." This was a lie; I had not eliminated my gag reflex, but I figured that if they insisted on a demonstration I could always say I was still three days away from being officially STD-free. The form also asked for my weight, and I wrote it down honestly, possibly for the last time in my life.

Once the co-captains of the squad, who introduced themselves as Horace and Javier, had collected all the forms, they led us over to the bleachers, where the coach, a queeny, moustachioed martinet the size of Tinker Bell, welcomed us to the clinic. His name was Christopher, he told us, though on the squad people referred to him as Princess. "But calling me Princess is a privilege," he continued sternly. "You have to *earn* the right to call me Princess."

He went on, but it became somewhat difficult to concentrate on what he was saying when a dozen guys and one woman in startlingly bright but uncampy uniforms (short-sleeved shirts and long pants for the men, a short halter top and a pleated skirt for the woman—all, lamentably, polyester, but I came to learn that this was standard fabric for cheerleading uniforms) began practicing behind him on the other side of the gym. My heart leapt within my breast to see a grown man jump into the hands of two other grown men who hurled him up into the air, where he executed a complex maneuver that had undoubtedly required years of study to master but that filled him in this moment with the grace and fire of a sub-Saharan predator or a bird long dead even to myth. Then he fell back down into his protectors' arms as if they had been formed to fit him.

Watching this, I became, if possible, even more determined than before to become a part of the squad. I tore my gaze away from the practice and unobtrusively surveyed the other homosexuals gathered around me. There were a couple of women and perhaps two dozen men, all of whom I hated. Who knew how many new squad members would be accepted? What if they were looking for ten new cheerleaders and I was number eleven? Two or three of the hopefuls were unspeakably beautiful and I hated them most of all. To my left in the row in front of me sat a gorgeous Latino with a Japanese character tattooed on his arm; I wanted him to ravish me and then die.

We started the tryouts, in which we had to perform complicated cheers like "Go, New York, let's go!" and "New York, let's hear it! Yell 'Go, fight, win!' " I spent the entire time with a look of grim concentration on my face, hoping that my cohorts would trip and fall while I got everything right. Every once in a while I would remember that I was supposed to be cheering and freeze my face in a rictus of joy for a minute or two. Then I would forget again and go back to using my psychic powers to give my competitors acute appendicitis.

At the end of the tryouts we were given the opportunity to show off any special skills we might have. Since I suspected that my proficiency in foreign languages wasn't particularly relevant to the duties I would be asked to perform as a cheerleader, and since, looking around, I thought it likely that *everybody* on the squad had long ago extinguished all traces of a gag reflex, the only thing left to display was my front handspring, which went beautifully until I landed and fell on my ass. Humiliated, I asked to try again; a lanky homosexual who looked to be about twelve years old grabbed my arm and hissed under his breath, "Lean forward when you land." I did, and I stayed upright. Figuring I should quit while I was at least not behind, I fled as soon as the tryouts were over. "Phone the hotline after noon tomorrow," called Princess as I made good my escape, "and there'll be a message with the names of the new squad members."

The next morning, I showed up trembling for my wretched day job. (I spent hours every weekday transcribing tapes of interviews in which people said things like, "Yeah, as I told you, we are a very vanilla house, even, as I told you, futures are mainly used to hedge some positions or to implement continuing duration strategies, but not as an important distinction or asset class." I did not know what any of this meant but it was clear to me that I was helping rich people become even richer while I had to pull out a calculator to see whether I could afford to buy peanut butter.) At the stroke of noon I tore off my headphones, ran to the phone, and dialed the Cheer New York hotline. My name was the third or fourth that Princess's voice lisped on the message, and the instant I heard it I began jumping up and down and running around the office shouting, "New York, let's hear it! Yell 'Go, fight, win!'" and doing toe touches. I tried to figure out a way to insert an *i* into my name so I could dot it with a heart, and I started making plans to be really mean to all the unpopular kids.

The next day, unfortunately, I had my first cheersetback. There are two cheerleading positions, flyer and base; flyers are the people who get thrown in the air and caught on the way down, and bases are the people who do the throwing and catching. On a traditional squad, the flyers are petite girls and the bases are burly boys. However, since there were only four girls on Cheer New York and only two of them were petite, we had to bend the rules a little bit and let men do some of the flying. I am under five-six and ~~140~~ 135 pounds, not as tiny as Princess or the bird long dead to myth, but still much smaller than most of the other guys on the squad, so I looked forward to lording my position as a flyer over rivals and loved ones alike. All my friends would be stuck on the ground and I would float above them.

Except that Cheer New York had assigned me to a new category, that of "mid-base flyer." In the e-mail Princess sent out to the squad informing us of our positions, he explained that mid-base flyers would indeed fly, but never above the bases' heads. I understood immediately that this meant he thought I was too fat to be thrown in the air. I sent a brittle response saying that I thought more useful positions to designate would be "top" and "bottom." Princess replied, "LOL!!!!!!! But seriously, we discourage squad members from sleeping with each other, for the benefit of team morale." And I was like, why the fuck didn't you mention this at the orientation?

That weekend there was an LGBT athletic team Christmas mixer, to which Cheer New York was invited, at a bar in Chelsea called XL. I hate bars with a deep and abiding hatred: they are loud, so I can't have a conversation; often smoky (depending upon city ordinances), so I can't breathe; and full of intimidating people with stylish haircuts, so I spend a lot of time in the corner repeating over and over the words "I will not die alone." I went to the mixer fully prepared to spend an anguished hour failing to mix with anybody before going home and eating a pound of M&M's.

Instead, I had a totally great time.

From the instant I walked in, the cheerleaders were so welcoming that I felt as if I were at a party with old friends where the music just happened to be too loud. It was also heartening to see that, of twenty-five squad members there, perhaps seven were white, a marked contrast to the racial segregation that pervades even the gay community. Furthermore, the cheerleaders were so flaming they could have melted granite. Nobody who spends more than three seconds in my company can say that I am a paragon of traditional masculinity. But next to some of these guys I was Arnold Schwarzenegger. And, to top it all off, there were presents: a "Cheer Loud, Cheer Proud" T-shirt, which I immediately put on and tied very tightly to expose my midriff, and a really gay silver sparkly Santa hat. The cheerleaders were the most touchy-feely group of which I have ever been a part, and within moments I was leaning all over people, hugging them, putting my hands in their pockets, and being swishier than I had allowed myself to

be in fifteen years of being out, sucking my teeth and saying
things like, "She's such a bitch!" while pointing dramatically at
a big, beefy man holding pom-poms and a cosmo.

It felt like home.

Two days later I went to my first cheerleading practice, and
it was a joy from start to finish. The ratio of bases to flyers was
off, so I learned the flyer parts, the first of which involved my
placing my hands on the shoulders of two rugged men named
Andy and Gian, leaping into their hands, and being lifted up so
that my feet were at the level of their chests. This was called a
half extension and it was terrifying.

It wasn't so much that I was so high up—I was maybe four
feet off the ground—as how unstable it felt. When you're on
a four-foot-high wall you can just walk along it as if you were
on the ground. But in Andy and Gian's hands, though the two
of them were doing exactly what they were supposed to do, I
might as well have been trying to balance in the middle of the
air on Jell-O. The rest of the squad was gathered around us, so
if things went awry I was unlikely to crack my head open, but
while my brain understood this my trembling body did not.

And then came the dismount: on Princess's cue, Andy and
Gian flung me up into the air, and I became briefly perhaps not
a sub-Saharan predator but still a creature I had never been before, bound not by the laws of physics but only by the reaches
of my own vision, which seemed in that instant fierce and lim-
itless. I hung for a heartbeat weightless and immortal, filled
with possibility, and then I fell.

I do not usually remember my dreams; when I do I find
that they have been stories of writing sequels to *Paradise Lost* in
ungrammatical French rebus, or of silencing my critics by producing a knitted model of the human brain and naming all its
parts correctly, or at least faking it in such a way that they don't

realize I have no idea what I'm talking about. On occasion I also dream, boringly, that I am falling. The instant before I hit the ground I wake up with a start, my heart racing and my eyes wild and my breath short, because what choice do I have but to die, if not tonight in my dream then tomorrow in an explosion or next year of a disease or at any moment of despair?

But here, in the middle of my first cheerleading practice, I found, miraculously, another choice, and it was: to be safe. Once they had thrown me in the air, Andy and Gian quickly crouched down and brought their hands together, creating a cushion for me to land on. And I have never loved anyone as much as I loved them in that moment, when I plummeted from what felt like infinite heights, eyes squeezed shut, not knowing whether there would be anything to keep me from slamming into the floor, and they caught me and cradled me as if my price were above rubies.

They bounced up and gently deposited me on the floor, and the rest of the squad, which had been hollering encouragement the whole time, exploded into cheers mixed with the occasional "You go, girl!" Walking home after practice I passed by a small flock of pigeons picking at crumbs on the sidewalk, and as I approached them they scattered and took wing. *That's me*, I thought with a smile, and decided that if I could go to cheerleading practice every day I would never need therapy again.

I was wrong, of course.

Oh, it was all fine to begin with. I was still enjoying myself a great deal when we performed for the Team New York awards ceremony, in a cramped but convivial room at the LGBT Community Center, and I continued to learn the flyer parts, ultimately mastering the half extension (with my eyes open, thank you) and the wolf wall. I also started taking gymnastics classes for the first time since the age of six and eventually produced a passable round-off back handspring, which we immediately added to our choreographed routine. We started cheering for the Sharks, New York's team in the Independent Women's Football League. This was a sight to behold: hordes of massive helmeted women tackling one another on the field while two dozen fey men cheered "O-O-O-Offense!" before realizing that our team was actually playing defense, at which point we switched to "D-D-D-Defense!" until we heard the unmistakable tinkling of the ice-cream truck around the corner and all sprinted to get Oreo Bars.

But gradually the nurturing quality of the group interactions was eclipsed by the fact that they were group interactions. The outpouring of love I had felt at XL was no match for my deadly fear of others, which, having left me alone for a time, now began to reassert itself. I started skipping squad outings to bars when I could, and when I couldn't I stood around for fifteen minutes nursing a Diet Coke while not talking to anybody and then ran away. Princess started berating me one day for not coming to the bar after the Sharks' most recent victory and in order to make him stop I told him I had a drinking problem. I felt increasingly alienated from the other squad members, because they had the body of Hercules or the grace of Midori Ito or the social life of Paris Hilton. True, I did finally get the Spirit Stick after months of hoping the people who received it instead of me would plummet from full extensions to their deaths on the gym floor. And at the season's-end dinner I was, bafflingly, given the Personality Award; I was so unprepared for this that when I opened my mouth to make an acceptance speech what came out was, "Ha! I've fooled you all!" which only confused people.

But then there were also things like the ski trip six of us took one February weekend to Horace's parents' house in the Poconos. It rained on Saturday, which meant that we couldn't ski; we were all relieved, the obligation to ski having been the only downside to the ski trip. So instead we went shopping at the outlet mall and I ate popcorn and bought a really cute bag. After such a successful day, though, I had to go and ruin every thing by accompanying the other cheerleaders to a gay bar. Even there things started out promisingly downstairs, where my virgin karaoke performance ("I Don't Know How to Love Him" from *Jesus Christ Superstar*) was a smashing success despite the song's being totally in the wrong key for me. Then I went upstairs to the bar and smiled at the handsome, shirtless bartender, who smiled back. Maybe my life wasn't a cruel joke the Fates had decided to play on me, I thought. Then cheerleader Robbie saw the handsome, shirtless bartender smiling at me and patted my shoulder condescendingly. "Oh, he does that to everybody," he said, and my soul shriveled into a little ball of self-hatred and despair. Robbie walked away, came back three minutes later, and said, "He asked me to meet him after close." I said, "Oh," and went into the bathroom and tried not to cry.

The evening got worse from there. Robbie, Mark, Steven, and Phil all got roaring drunk (Horace and I weren't drinking—I because I don't, he because he had to drive), and Mark and Robbie started dancing shirtless in the go-go cage, clearly having more fun doing so than all the fun I had ever had in my entire life put together. I watched them in agony for a time, torn between my desperate desire to join them and actually enjoy myself for one second and my mortal terror of joining them and making myself a laughingstock. Eventually the former impulse won out; I bravely took my shirt off and joined them in the go-go cage, where I felt like an idiot because there wasn't enough room for three people and I moved as gracefully as a Parkinsonian C-3PO.

I gyrated halfheartedly for two minutes, during which time I was so miserable I wanted to put my eyes out with a carving fork, and then I got out of the go-go cage. Eventually the four drunk cheerleaders played out an intensely annoying drama about who was taking which strangers home and who was avoiding taking which strangers home, and in the end nobody took any strangers home. I puttered around the house briefly before going up to my room only to find Phil there giving Mark a blow job. I took this as my cue to find somewhere else to sleep and made up the air mattress downstairs. Then I puttered around for a while longer, helping Horace clean and rolling my eyes with him at the drunken behavior of the other four. I was grateful for the shared moment with somebody I liked and respected. Our bond was already infinitely deeper than the shallow fun the drunk cheerleaders were having, and it deepened further when Horace loaned me his copy of *Emma* as bedtime reading.

Then I woke up the next morning to learn that after I'd fallen asleep he'd gone upstairs to fuck Steven for an hour and a half.

Events like this took their toll on my cheerleading. At Pride appearances and Sharks games I grinned and clapped and round-off back handsprang as maniacally as ever, but home felt farther and farther away. No one ever dropped me from a half extension (though I did give Tommy a black eye once during a twist-down) but the rapture of trusting in the hands of others to support me became ever more elusive. I couldn't understand: I was doing everything right, yet the promise of that bright Thanksgiving morning was growing emptier week by week.

Nonetheless, I might still have been okay if it hadn't been for the transcranial magnetic stimulation.

Anything resembling a complete history of the decline and fall of my mental health would quickly become so soporific as to send a meth addict into a coma. Suffice it to say that I was more or less all right until the age of twenty, at which point my multifarious anxiety disorders broke free from the chains that had bound them and began to ruin my life.

I can't stand it when people laughingly say things like, "I got all OCD about filling out that form" when what they mean is, "I filled out that form more punctiliously than necessary." Obsessive-compulsive disorder is something completely different (not to mention being a noun rather than an adjective). When people have OCD, their minds are filled with intrusive, irrational, repetitive thoughts often so frightening as to render them incapable of concentrating on anything else, and they end up performing rituals to ward off whatever those thoughts make them afraid of, even though they are perfectly aware their fears are groundless. One of the most common obsessions, for example, is a fear that everything around you is contaminated. This is usually paired with a compulsion to wash your hands. People who feel this compulsion strongly can wash their hands until they bleed, and keep on washing—knowing all the while that what they are doing makes absolutely no sense.

Another disorder on the OCD spectrum, rarer but just as

fun, is Tourette's syndrome. Among other things, this can cause people to call out random words (often obscenities) with no apparent stimulus.

I have neither classical obsessive-compulsive disorder nor classical Tourette's syndrome, but an ambiguous combination of the two. Instead of obsessing about germs and compulsively washing my hands, or shouting "motherfucker!" every three seconds, when I am under stress I am mentally assailed by hate slurs—racist, anti-Semitic, sexist, homophobic, any other -ist or -ic you care to name.

There's a reason they call OCD the waking nightmare. I grew up with parents who had devoted their lives to the cause of civil rights; my favorite person to spend time with as a child was our neighbor Septima Clark, who had trained Rosa Parks in tactics of nonviolent protest. And in my worst periods it's as if the Ku Klux Klan had erected a burning cross not on my lawn but in my mind. If I can see a photograph of Leontyne Price, the most glorious opera singer the world has ever known, whose debut at the Metropolitan Opera earned her a standing ovation that lasted *forty-two minutes,* whose voice in concert has made me hyperventilate and whose artistry has been an inspiration to me since before I can remember, and be powerless to prevent the words "nigger bitch" from battering my consciousness over and over and over and over and over and over and over until they level every thought in my head, not just every idea about bills I have to pay or lunch I have to eat but in the end every understanding of hope and love and belief my body can contain—well, then, it would be better to be dead; it would be better to be dead and in hell.

Thankfully, my worst periods are few and very far between—only two or three in the last fifteen years—but when you start with the fact that, upon occasion, seeing Harvey Fierstein in a movie causes the phrase "faggot kike" to seize control of my brain, and add 1) a crippling social phobia that renders me incapable of asking drugstore clerks where the protein bars are for fear they will snort at me in derision and mock me after I leave the store, and 2) a generalized anxiety that means the last time I felt completely relaxed was for about twenty minutes on the morning of February 6, 2001, as well as 3) a need to take sips from water fountains in multiples of four or go mad with discomfort—four sets of nine sips is best but if there are people behind me I don't want to risk angering them and so I can make do with four sets of five or, in extraordinary cases, four sets of three, though any lower than that and I have to do two sets of four sets of sips—what you end up with is a person who is sometimes not in such great shape.

Medication worked wonders for a time but eventually lost its efficacy and, since standing at the edge of the subway platform in case I realized as the train was coming that I needed to jump was not my idea of a good time, I decided to investigate other possible treatments. Unfortunately, homeopathic remedies did nothing; acupuncture did nothing; a faith healer did nothing (shut up, I was desperate). I ran across credible reports suggesting that psychedelic mushrooms have anti-OCD properties, and so, despite the fact that the eighth-grade assembly on drug addiction had frightened me so much I had never even smoked a cigarette, I decided to grow some shrooms. Sadly, the attempt coincided with a mouse infestation in my building, and the mice ate the shrooms before I could harvest them, which meant that I had OCD *and* an apartment full of tripping mice.

So when I read about a New York–based study of a new technique called transcranial magnetic stimulation, I was intrigued. This was shortly after I started to lose my enthusiasm for cheerleading; maybe I could get it back, I thought, if I recalibrated my brain.

In many people with psychiatric problems, goes the idea behind TMS, certain areas of the brain are sluggish or hyperactive, but by aiming electromagnetic pulses at those areas, you can speed them up or slow them down. This is not electroconvulsive therapy, in which doctors anesthetize a patient and then send an electric shock through his or her entire brain strong enough to induce a seizure; TMS is much less drastic and more targeted.

The only problem was that I didn't actually have the illness the study was investigating. The doctors were looking for people with major depressive disorder—the kind that can prevent you from feeding yourself and sometimes from bathing—and whatever was going on in my brain, it wasn't that. Furthermore, people with OCD were specifically excluded, and though I didn't have classical OCD, what I did have was certainly close enough to disqualify me.

However, I had exhausted all my other options, so I just signed up and lied through my teeth. True, they would be aiming the magnets at parts of my brain associated with a disorder I didn't have, but hey, I thought, it's not as if I can get any *worse,* so what do I have to lose?

At my entrance interview I therefore exaggerated my depressive symptoms as much as I could and left out my obsessive ones entirely. One of the first questions they asked, for example, was whether I woke up earlier than I needed to and whether, if so, I could go back to sleep. I did in fact wake up earlier than I needed to, generally at around eight or nine, which for people in the theater is the middle of the night, but I didn't think that would be convincing enough, so I told them I usually woke up between four and six and was unable to get to sleep again. There were about thirty of these diagnostic questions, all of which I answered as haltingly as I could, dulling my affect and crying the first chance I got. That night they called me and said I was eligible for the study and could I start on Monday and I said yes definitely.

This turned out to be a bad idea.

First of all, TMS was very boring. I went every weekday over the course of two and a half months and sat in a chair for forty-five minutes with a machine the size of a large stereo component at my back. A flexible tube connected the machine to a little plastic hat, which sat just above the hairline on the left side of my head. Twice a minute, electromagnetic pulses from the plastic hat would poke at my scalp like a manic woodpecker for several seconds. The pulses were slightly painful for the first few minutes of the first day, but after that my nerve endings got used to them. The study protocol forbade me to read or fall asleep, and my head was immobilized, so I ended up staring at the Monet print on the wall and contemplating my own existence. This was not fun.

And what's more, it didn't do me any good. In fact, showing up every day and lying only made me exponentially more anxious. Compounding this anxiety was the repeat interview I had every two weeks; with each one it became increasingly difficult for me to keep track of my previous answers. *Crap*, I would think, *did I tell them last time that I had spent less than three hours a day in productive activity the previous week, or that I had spent more than three hours a day in productive activity but had had thoughts or feelings of incapacity, fatigue, or weakness?* Soon enough I *was* waking up between four and six every morning and unable to get back to sleep, but I couldn't figure out whether to say that I was waking up between four and six every morning, which now had the virtue of being true, or that I was waking up between two and four every morning, which had the virtue of indicating that I was getting worse, which was also true. I ended up deciding on the latter, in case they could turn up the voltage or use a secret backup protocol that would *really* fix me, though I did worry that if my trajectory didn't change I would soon have to claim to be waking up at eight-thirty in the evening. Unfortunately, they did not turn up the voltage, and if there was a secret backup protocol they never used it on me.

Before long the anxiety I had previously felt was as naught; I was filled with such terrifying dread every time the phone rang or someone asked me a question or I picked up a spoon that I became almost incapable of speech. Every morning, after sitting bolt upright at five with my heart pounding and unable to breathe, I cried for an hour and a half before waking my boyfriend up to comfort me—he *loved* this—until one day the understanding came crashing onto me in an instant that he wasn't good enough for me (a medical student and a painter, he regularly said things like, "I can't decide whether I want to join Doctors Without Borders after I graduate or run a gay community health center"). Since I couldn't bear the guilt of keeping secrets, I faithfully reported this understanding and all its permutations to him. For a month and a half I would call him and he would say "Hi, how are you?" and I would say something like "I'm really anxious because I met somebody today I was very attracted to and I think you and I shouldn't be together and that I should be dating a millionaire who speaks eight languages" and he would say "Okay, well, can we talk about that when we see each other tonight?" and when we saw each other that night I would sit in silence and watch episodes of *Law & Order,* not new ones because I couldn't pay enough attention to take anything in, but old ones I'd already seen, but not old ones with Benjamin Bratt or Jesse L. Martin because the OCD was haunting me with a vengeance and I preferred to avoid situations that would fill my brain with racist slurs, and then my boyfriend would say "So do you want to talk about what you said earlier?" and I would say "No" and pace around the apartment hitting myself in the face and then I would fall asleep and sit bolt upright at five the next morning with my heart pounding and unable to breathe and start the whole thing over again except for the time when I decided the reason I had felt a little better after my last TMS session must have been that beforehand I'd taken a Benadryl at two in the morning and so I stayed up until two in the morning again and took another Benadryl and stared at the ceiling wishing I had never been born until it was time to get up.

This interfered somewhat with my ability to be an effective cheerleader.

I could still plaster the simulacrum of a smile onto my face, and I could still yell "Go, New York, let's go!" But it took all my willpower to do even this much. I was able to wrench about 5 percent of my attention to eating and bathing and gesturing with pom-poms—all of which activities now required huge expenditures of psychic energy—while the rest of my brain devoured itself like an ouroboros. How could I put any real effort into a half extension when my mind was torturing itself to death?

And it wasn't just the impossibility of concentration and the wishing I had never been born that got in the way (and the fever pitch my OCD reached in the midst of such a multi-ethnic group as Cheer New York); physical obstacles began to arise as well. At one practice I finally threw a round-off back tuck, which I celebrated by throwing three more, falling, and breaking my left hand. This meant that I had to cheerlead in the Gay Pride Parade in a cast. I was delighted to have suffered an actual sports injury and, even better, to have physical proof thereof. But after the cast came off, I no longer trusted my body, and I was never able to tumble with quite the same élan.

And then something else unexpected began to happen: heterosexual girls started joining the squad. As a rule I adore heterosexual girls, but these particular ones were three feet tall and twelve inches around, so when they joined they became flyers. This meant that I sat more and more often on the sidelines, watching as Laura and Katie and then Melanie and then Jessica were hurled higher into the air than I had ever reached. I hated Laura and Katie and Melanie and Jessica for this. I hated them even more because they had all been cheerleaders in college. *You had your chance already,* I thought bitterly. *Why are you taking mine away?* I tried basing once or twice, so as not to feel completely useless, but since I was all of two inches taller and thirteen pounds heavier than the actual flyers, my efforts did not inspire confidence. On top of this, the new flyers were all engaged in noble, self-sacrificing pursuits, so eventually I spent my practices bubbling over with venom for cute girls who worked in extended-care facilities for the developmentally disabled and spent their free time volunteering at homeless shelters. I leapt into nobody's hands and nobody cradled me. Flying was for other people; I was earthbound.

Meanwhile, I finally felt so guilty about my manipulation of the TMS study that I confessed the truth to the doctors running it, who were unfazed. "Oh, okay," they said. "That happens all the time. We design the studies to take it into account." I sobbed with relief for three hours and the next morning I slept until six-thirty.

I went back on medication, and my anxiety and OCD subsided somewhat, and I no longer felt as if my body might fly apart at the slightest provocation. But I was a broken man. I lay on the couch in a blanket all day watching television and eating chocolate and unable to motivate myself, no matter how hard I tried, to pick up the piece of scrap paper on the floor by the window. I turned down every invitation I received. I didn't answer the phone. I gave up cooking, I stopped going to the gym, I wrote nothing. I tried to make a will so I could commit suicide, but the whole process required far more energy than I was able to summon, so I gave up; I was too depressed to kill myself. Then I decided my medication was actually making me feel worse so I stopped taking it but didn't tell my psychiatrist or my boyfriend. My final effort to feel better had failed, and now the only choice I had left was to live the rest of my life in unceasing torment.

I took a leave of absence from the cheerleading squad. I couldn't bear watching other people soar through the air while I was unable to stop falling. Princess called and e-mailed several times to ask how I was doing but I did not answer his messages. Finally he sent me an e-mail that said, "I thought we were friends and I am OFFENDED at your actions. I've tried to get in touch MANY TIMES and you have never responded, so I will assume you don't want to be on the squad anymore and I am REMOVING you from the squad list!!!!! Love, Princess." I felt a dull twinge somewhere deep in my small intestine that resembled the ache I get when I find out I have made somebody angry at me, but mostly I was just relieved that my life had become even smaller.

(Though when I complained to my friend Jen about being kicked off the squad, she said, "Well, you weren't actually kicked off the squad. You were just mean to it until it broke up with you.")

Eventually I began to ease out of my despair, at least a little bit. I went to a birthday party for a friend and had a shadow of a good time. I switched psychiatrists, went back on medication, started writing again, returned a few calls. It took a Herculean effort to drag myself to the gym, but every once in a while I made it for my favorite aerobics class. I cooked my boyfriend dinner a couple times. I knitted a sweater for a collaborator's newborn son. I bought a garbage can. Small accomplishments, yes, but when you are at the bottom of a pit, any movement toward the light is a victory.

A year passed, and my days were no longer the bleak emptiness they had seemed for a time. And I figured that, if I no longer wanted to throw myself in front of *every* passing subway train, then I had to be doing something right.

But I couldn't go back to Cheer New York. One late October afternoon I sat down to draft an e-mail to Princess and explain the whole thing to him, but, as soon as I typed the salutation, the pixellated Garamond characters on my computer screen rearranged themselves to depict cheerleaders laughing and tumbling and sucking their teeth and the hateful Laura and Katie and Melanie and Jessica cheering altruistically and Andy and Gian about to throw somebody else into the air. I stared at the blank e-mail window for a long time and then I shut my computer off and went outside to get a Diet Mountain Dew.

As I walked toward the drugstore on the corner I looked up and saw several pigeons roosting in one of the trees lining the street. They looked at one another every once in a while but they didn't coo and they didn't fly anywhere. I stopped to watch them—according to the cashiers I was the only person who ever bought Diet Mountain Dew so it's not like I was worried it would sell out—but they stayed put. I watched them for a long time and occasionally one of them took a couple steps or hopped a little bit but none of them left the tree, and I couldn't decide whether it was because they didn't want to or because they couldn't. Eventually the sun set but I stood rooted to the sidewalk, looking up in the dark at the birds I could no longer see. Finally I went back home and went to sleep. I dreamed that I was falling, and in the dream my eyes were shut tight, because I didn't want to open them and see that there was no one there to catch me.

On Camp Camp

One afternoon near the middle of summer, the counselors at the Jewish Community Center Day Camp announced that the next day would be Backwards Day and that, in order to express our wild sides (we were six), we should show up dressed as unusually as possible. I could barely contain my excitement; I instantly began a mental list of funny ways to wear my clothing, and by the time I got home my parents had to talk me out of altering my mother's wedding dress to make a pair of long, trailing socks.

I had thus far led a disappointingly typical camp experience—friends, rivals, crushes, just like everybody else—but I was growing increasingly uncomfortable with this state of affairs. I belonged in the center of attention. My attempt to get there by convincing my animal group to change its name from the Eagles to the South American Giant Anacondas had been thwarted by the other children's cowardice, but I realized that with a striking enough Backwards Day ensemble I could thrust myself into the spotlight without needing to rely on anybody else. I got to camp the next day with my shirt on inside out, my hair disheveled and sprayed to immobility, my father's shoes on the wrong feet, my mother's makeup covering my face in bright geometric patterns, and my pants hiked up far enough to risk future sterility, only to find all the other kids wearing normal clothes. I'd misunderstood the counselors' instructions; Backwards Day wasn't until the next day, and today we were going on a field trip to the zoo.

The geometrically applied makeup almost hid the flush of my mortification. The other children didn't act any differently than they usually did, but I knew that inside they were shrieking with laughter. At the bus's first rest stop, one of the counselors helped me put my shirt on right side out and wiped the blush off my face. But my father's shoes still dwarfed my feet, and my hair remained implacably stiff, and there was nothing to be done about the mascara. When we got to the zoo I gazed at the sullen hippopotamus and wished I could trade bodies with it in a feat of transmigratory sorcery, but the hippopotamus declined to cooperate, and when we went home at the end of the day I did not know how to face my parents and tell them what a failure I was.

One would think I had learned my lesson, but two weeks later I showed up a day early for Fifties Day, in a white T-shirt with a pack of my mother's Merit Ultra Lights rolled into the shoulder and my hair slicked into a ducktail with an Elvis curl at the front.

Eventually camp ended and I went back to school, where I felt more at ease, because facts about the Paleolithic Era remained the same whether it was Wednesday or Thursday and whether I was dying inside or not. But even as the agony of Backwards Day began to fade I swore that before returning to any summer camp I would spend my vacation at a leper colony.

Unfortunately, I hadn't counted on the stained glass.

One day a couple of years ago my friend Jennifer opened a drawer in her bureau and produced a stunning multicolored window and told me her girlfriend Lisa had made it at Camp Camp, a weeklong summer camp in Maine for gay people (and lesbians and bisexuals and transsexuals). I had not forgotten my leper-colony vow, but the stained glass ensorceled me; the integrity of my word was no match for the shiny colors. I would have done anything to be able to make such a window. I would have eaten dirt; I would have spoken to a child. Going to summer camp, therefore, was a burden I was happy to bear. Nevertheless, a part of me remained wary. Twenty-four years had passed since my JCC debacle, but what if the nightmare simply repeated itself? What if it was worse? Furthermore, this was sleepaway camp, so I didn't even have the option of coming home and crying and putting on a brave face the next morning; it would be one continuous horror.

Jennifer tried to allay my fears. "We're totally going back," she said. "It's a little bit like a cult. A warm and fuzzy cult. Everybody is incredibly happy to be there. It's so supportive and positive."

These words filled me with dread. In intimate conversation I am as supportive and positive as the next man, but gatherings of happy people make me miserable. I long to share in the collective joy, but instead I am racked with anxiety; this makes me feel with an exquisite keenness my sense of alienation from my fellow human beings and from the universe itself. It also makes me feel fat. Set such a gathering in a place with no air-conditioning or cable television and what you have is something akin to the burning wheel on which Ixion turns forever in Hades. But I figured that with enough Ativan I could get through anything, so I filled out the online form, sent in my fee, and crossed my fingers that everything would be all right.

Upon my arrival at the campsite, I made my way to my cabin, which was an actual log cabin that I had to walk through actual nature to get to, and saw a sign on the front that read BAR-NEY FRANK. All the Camp Camp cabins were named after famous homosexuals: Oscar Wilde, Walt Whitman, Audre Lorde, Xena (technically not a homosexual), Tom Cruise (technically not a—oh, wait). I had not entered a log cabin for a quarter of a century; this one featured three-inch foam mattresses resting on slats of plywood. I claimed a bed, the bottom of a bunked pair, and was sorry to see that its previous (adolescent) occupants had not scrupled at graffiti. "Jenny thinks Bianca is cool!" one girl had scrawled in black marker. Next to it I read, "Emily thinks Bianca is cool too!" Another girl had written, "Bianca is hot sex in a bottle!" and despite the bubbly circle dotting the *i*, I suspected that here was someone who might grow up to be a Camp Camper herself. Off to the side I saw, in a different color, an understated "Ashley slept here." I pictured Ashley, trying to fall asleep at night, listening to Jenny and Emily compete for Bianca's favor and wondering why she had been fated to be the outsider. I hoped she would end up running a Fortune 500 company and that Jenny, Emily, and Bianca would take to drink in a vain effort to preserve their fading looks.

Other men began arriving at the cabin. The prospect of meeting them frightened me, so I pretended to be asleep. They introduced themselves to one another—I quieted my feigned snoring enough to hear their names—as Steve, Steve, Michael, James, David (also a first-time camper), Steve, and Michael. (I am not making this up. Everyone at Camp Camp was named Michael, David, or Steve.) Their easy banter soon gave rise to the following exchange:

MICHAEL: I need a pillow.

DAVID: Didn't you bring one?

JAMES: Where would he have room for a pillow in that bag? He wouldn't have been able to fit his costume for the square dance.

DAVID: There's a square dance? Did you bring a hoop skirt?

MICHAEL: (*lisping*) I'm *so* much butcher than that.

Nothing in their words or manner was at all intimidating, and yet I hated David for dropping himself into the conversation so easily while I was paralyzed, like a stroke victim unable to move but still torturously aware of everything going on around him.

Before long Steve, Steve, Michael, James, David, Steve, and Michael left for dinner. Released from my state of suspended animation, I spent ten minutes agonizing over what to wear before realizing that every sweater I had brought looked terrible with my shoes. I gave up and ran to join the others in the main lodge.

I had a good time through most of dinner, actually; I sat with Steve, Steve, James, Michael, two other men named Kerry and Bryant, and two women named Eden and Clink. In between bites of salade Niçoise—this was gay camp, after all—I said many funny things at which they all laughed appreciatively. Then I saw Steve (or maybe it was Steve?) get up to go look at the desserts on offer, and I got up with him. After a few yards, however, he turned and I realized that I had misread the situation and that he was in fact on his way not to the dessert tray but to the bathroom. I blushed hideously and looked back and forth, helpless, between the desserts and my table. I understand that for many people this situation would not have presented a problem, but I felt as if my life hung in the balance: if I went one way my faux pas would rest eternally undiscovered and if I went the other way no one would ever care about me again—but I couldn't figure out which way was which. Finally I stumbled back toward the table, sat down, and hoped that my companions would fail to notice my mistake until enough time had passed that they could no longer reasonably hold me in contempt for my stupidity, or at the very least that anybody who did notice would immediately choke on an anchovy and die.

I guess it could have been worse, I thought as I picked up my fork. *This could have happened in front of Suzanne Hutchinson.*

A few weeks before my seventeenth birthday I made the bold decision to throw myself a party. I had never thrown a party before, so when I mailed cards to all fifty-three of my high school classmates inviting them to my house two weeks from Sunday I felt a rush of excitement. We would eat cake and chips and watch movies and laugh and talk into the wee hours of the morning and I would finally have friends.

It wasn't that nobody liked me. My classmates and I had not sworn vendetta against one another. But I did not spend time at their houses, nor they at mine; we did not call one another on the telephone except to ask about class assignments; I did not meet them on the weekend for spirited games of tag football. But now, with one dramatic move, I was going to effect a sea change. This party would celebrate not only my birthday but also my entry into the world of humans.

Or so I thought until the next day, when Matthew Gibson announced that he was throwing a party two weeks from Sunday.

I couldn't reschedule, as the invitations had already gone out. So I simply spent the next two weeks pretending that

Matthew Gibson didn't exist. I didn't ask people whether they would be at my party; I just willed myself to believe they were coming. I bought a backseatful of Tostitos and Lay's and Coke, and on Saturday I filled a Tupperware container with chocolate chip cookies I baked from a tube of Pillsbury Dough Boy chocolate chip cookie dough, and used my mother's Cuisinart stand mixer to make a Duncan Hines devil's-food cake that I frosted painstakingly with a jar of Duncan Hines chocolate frosting. The afternoon of the day I had chosen I decorated the house and arranged the bowls of Tostitos and Lay's in aesthetically pleasing configurations and sat down and waited, and three people came.

Three.

Julie, Allison, Kathy, and I sat around acting as if nothing were amiss. We ate cake and chips and watched a movie, just like I'd planned, but the stench of humiliation overpowered any impulse to laugh, and there was no talking into the wee hours of the morning because as soon as the movie was over they all went home, and I did not have friends.

Under the covers that night, I wept into my pillow until merciful sleep overtook me. The next morning, however, I walked into homeroom with my head held high, humming "Non, je ne regrette rien," fiercely determined not to show the slightest hint of pain. I was wounded, yes, but it would take a lot more than the previous night's events to strike the deathblow. And then Suzanne Hutchinson turned around and saw me and said, "Hey, Joel, I heard you had a really bitchin' party last night!"

I am certain that she intended only an easy score, that she was not trying to sear a moment into my mind that I would never be able to forget. But sixteen years later I can still see the perfectly straight hair and little round glasses that made her look like a cartoon owl, and the desk she was in—back row, second from the left—and the angle at which her upper body was turned as she spoke. In a daze I sat down in my front-row desk, feeling like a dog whose owner has slammed the pet gate shut in its face to keep it out of the room, and pretended that Mrs. Chanson was the only person in the world as she began a discussion of the Blake poem we had read over the weekend. "To see a World in a Grain of Sand/And a Heaven in a Wild Flower,/Hold Infinity in the palm of your hand/And Eternity in an hour," she quoted. *An hour already feels like eternity,* I thought, *when the palm of your hand holds nothing.*

I would be surprised now to find that Suzanne Hutchinson had any recollection at all of the crushing thing she said that day. And this makes me worry about the crushing things *I've* said of which I have no recollection. I already worry all the time about the crushing things I've said of which I *do* have a recollection, like when I told Melissa Tsai in college that Adam Feinman was a human petri dish, and he found out and he was really hurt, when what I actually meant was that I was jealous of him for having lots of sex, or when I tossed a note to Jon Reeves in seventh-grade Latin about how Theo Moore sucked and Theo caught it and read it, and how do you recover from doing something like that to somebody, especially when Theo is one of the two total losers in your grade, the other one being Chip Safell, and you're especially vicious simply because you know how narrowly you've escaped their fate? I went over to Theo's house to hang out a couple times and his mother adored me because I was one of God's Chosen People, and shortly after he submitted an original drawing of Zeus to the Latin Forum competition and won a prize I was in his room and saw that he had actually copied it from a magazine cover and I didn't know what to say. Theo left school before too long, followed in short order by Chip, and I don't know what happened to him, but thinking about him today makes me queasy because it reminds me that whatever was in Suzanne is in me too.

So if that's how I feel about the moments that have lingered in my memory, what about the moments I've forgotten? Who among my former acquaintance is at this moment recalling the day in high school when I turned halfway around in my seat and inadvertently pierced every pretense he had constructed that he wasn't an unhappy alien? In whose face did I slam the gate?

Dinner on the first night of Camp Camp was not the only meal I found stressful. Throughout the week, no matter who I sat with, inside of thirty seconds I looked up and saw other people sitting elsewhere who I thought were cooler. No matter that if I'd sat with them to begin with I would have looked up at the people I was sitting with now and thought *they* were cooler; I was incapable of choosing correctly. At lunch on Tuesday I found a seat across from two men I had met in the stained-glass studio whose names were almost certainly David and Steve. As I lifted my glass of fruit punch to my lips, I saw Kerry and James—both in Barney Frank with me—sitting a few tables over. I knew that if I abandoned David and Steve for them, they would envelop me in the radiance of their coolness and make me belong and I would be happy, but I couldn't bring myself to hurt David's and Steve's feelings, so I resigned myself to being miserable but polite until I died. At another table I saw two men who were less cool than I—the haircuts alone would have been enough—and it occurred to me that I could go over and envelop them in the radiance of what little coolness I had at my disposal. But then I realized that this would take me even further away from the truly cool people, who would think even less of me than I knew they already did.

When I walked into the main lodge that night for the Karaoke Lounge, however, I brimmed with hope. I intended to scan the tables, find the coolest people I knew, and cling to them as fiercely as Kate Winslet clings to the splintered piece of flotsam in *Titanic* while Leonardo DiCaprio dies of hypothermia. I would not feel comfortable, certainly; all the same, at least I would have a moment of respite from the unceasing struggle not to drown.

But it was not to be. Every cool person was already engaged in conversation with another cool person, and I saw no way to breach the walls those conversations had erected. So I made my way to an empty bench at the side of the room. Better I should spend the evening in lonely isolation than that I should be surrounded by people with no one but myself for company.

Then the karaoke started. Vickers, the head lifeguard, sang "I Write the Songs (That Make the Whole World Sing)." She was dressed in a bright orange shirt and overall shorts; she didn't move and her eyes never left the karaoke screen, yet she sang so proudly that I couldn't help loving her. When she got to the key change the audience burst into applause. Then she finished and I remembered that I was alone.

I saw Ryan the cute lifeguard and stood up to go sit with him but when I got closer I saw that Kerry was sitting right behind him, arms around him and chin in the crook of his neck. I veered away, cringing at my desire to belong and wanting to strike myself, and walked back to my empty bench. I hated them both and myself most of all.

Then Bill Cole, who had founded Camp nine years earlier, came onstage in excruciating drag. On our first day in Maine, Bill had told us about the birth of Camp Camp. "I came out to my wife when I was forty-nine," he said, "and she put me on a bus to Provincetown. The people I saw there were beautiful and handsome, and I was like, I don't belong here. So I wanted to make a place where everybody could feel like they belonged." That afternoon I had looked around the room and wondered how many people there thought of themselves as beautiful and handsome. I wondered whether there were people in the room who thought of *me* as beautiful and handsome. I wondered how many beautiful and handsome people actually felt like they belonged.

Tonight, for the Karaoke Lounge, Bill had donned a purple A-line skirt, a glittery black top with two shawls—one peach, one silver—and a tangled ratty gray wig. He sang "Build Me Up, Buttercup" like an adorable lunatic. He had no conception of how to sing or move, and he got lost every line. "He does that every year," James told me afterward. "He knows it doesn't work, but he can't figure out why."

After the karaoke finally ended, I found myself talking with Bill about our childhoods. "When I was a little boy," he said, "there was this older guy, and he spent a lot of time at our house—I think he had a crush on my dad. He was very flamboyant, but I have no idea where he got it from. The town was tiny, there certainly weren't any models for him to follow. Did he just make it up out of nowhere? He had a really hairy chest and a gold chain. He played piano like Liberace and I was terrified of him. Eventually some kids bludgeoned him to death with a baseball bat." Bill was very matter-of-fact as he related this. "Even now, I'm not attracted to guys who are flamboyant, and I just know it's because of him."

And I thought, that's what has always happened to people who try to fit in where they're told they don't belong, isn't it? The baseball bat, the rope and the tree, the gas.

When I was in seventh grade, a sign appeared one day in an empty window on Charleston's main shopping street that read OPENING SOON: CACAO'S HANDMADE CHOCOLATES. Since I understood even at the tender age of thirteen that chocolate was the elixir of life, I rushed to the store after school the day it opened and bubbled at the proprietors, Mark and Rob, until they were forced to show me around. The shop was filled with what could only have been alchemical equipment, and the odors heavy in the air worked an enchantment on me more powerful than any spell Circe ever wrought. Even the words Mark and Rob used to describe what they did sounded magical: couverture, conching, theobroma.

Over the next two years I spent many of my free hours at Cacao's, and for the first time in a long while I knew something of what it felt like to be understood. Since my peers and I did not seek out one another's company, I was drawn to my teachers, and many of them found me amusing, but even if they regarded me as anything but a precocious child, the constraints of professionalism prevented them from more than a friendly acquaintance. Here in Cacao's, however, for the first time, I met adults who seemed to want to be my friends. They answered my questions without condescension or comment about my age and they listened to my opinions with what appeared to be respect. Rob was straight but Mark, I came to learn, was gay, as were many of the men and women who might be found chatting with him of an afternoon, and they welcomed me into their company (though I didn't yet understand how much we had in common). No tinge of sexuality ever colored our interactions; these people simply talked about interesting things and declined to patronize me when I chimed in. They were older than I, and their concerns were different, but the way they treated me revealed a glimpse of the camaraderie my future might hold.

Oddly, in Charleston my biggest problem fitting in wasn't being gay; it was being smart. Ever since well-educated carpet-baggers came south after the Civil War and hoodwinked former Confederates out of their land and their money and their political power, many Southerners have felt they have good reason to be suspicious of education. That's why states below the Mason-Dixon Line spend less money on schools and have lower literacy rates than the rest of the country: a citizenry so raised may or may not be undereducated, but at least it will be less likely to swindle you when you are desperate.

Of course, many Charlestonians would have found my civil-rights-worker parents untrustworthy even without the benefit of education. One afternoon when I was five I came home from playing with my across-the-street neighbor Betsy and asked my father, "Daddy, what's a nigger-loving kike?" When he recovered from the apoplectic fit into which this had sent him and asked me why I wanted to know, I said, "Because Betsy says that her daddy says that you are one."

Betsy's daddy also published a white-supremacist newsletter, though I didn't know that at the time. But I did know I was unlikely to join the ranks of the Good Ol' Boys. My mother's ancestors had settled the city and we were white, so most of our neighbors welcomed us heartily enough, but something in me still felt out of place bobbing for apples at the block Hallowe'en parties.

The one part of Charleston in which education found an enthusiastic home was the Jewish community, which is large, Charleston having been home to the first Reform congregation in America. But here too there was a problem; to wit, my mother was Christian. According to Jewish law, therefore, even though I was being raised Jewish, I was not considered a Jew by birth. I rectified this state of affairs at the age of seven by converting to Judaism. Nevertheless I lacked the strong points of reference that the other synagogue kids took for granted in their culturally Jewish homes.

Oh, my mother tried, but she exposed herself time and again, like when her mother-in-law tasted her matzo ball soup and said, her Polish accent unsoftened by forty years in America, "This is good, Mary Frances, but you need to work on your matzo balls. They're too fluffy. They should be heavy, like a rock." I felt certain no one had ever had to say this to Randy Kurtz's mother. How could I feel at home among people whose uncles were named Irving and Sol when mine was named Bubba?

And so, ill at ease with both the Southerners and the Jews, I found a group of like-minded people in a chocolate store; with the onset of puberty, as my sexual impulses blossomed, I realized just how like-minded we were. Finally one day in the preparation room a couple of Mark's friends kissed each other on the mouth, something I had never seen two men do before. I couldn't get the image out of my mind. Three days later I stopped by the store after school, as usual, and hung out while Mark enrobed things and unmolded other things and was jolly. And I waited and waited and waited to get up the courage to say what I wanted to say and I finally did but I was so scared I couldn't do it in English so I used French. *"J'ai peur que je suis gay,"* I said, failing in my nervousness to use the subjunctive. *I'm scared that I'm gay.*

Mark cocked his head and narrowed his eyes. "Let's sit down," he said, and we did. "If you made love to a man, what would be the best part?"

"Um . . . lying together afterward."

"And when you saw those two kissing the other day, what did you think?"

I wasn't brave enough to tell him I wished it had been me, so I just said, "I liked it."

We talked a little more, and he said, "Yes, you're gay," and I was flooded with a sense of homecoming. It is obvious to me in retrospect that he had understood this about me from the moment we met, but I appreciate his pretense of open-minded investigation. And thank *God* he didn't feed me any claptrap about how being attracted to boys didn't necessarily mean anything one way or another and as I grew older I would feel a lot of different things and I didn't need to make any decisions about who I was right away and blah blah blah because if he had said those things I would have felt more estranged from the world than ever and God knows what would have become of me by now.

As I mounted my bike to go home, Mark stood in front of the store and reached a hand toward me in benediction. "May Zeus be forever by your throne and Zephyr at your heels," he called, and I pedaled off, humming and grinning a huge grin.

For a while it looked like we in Barney Frank would emerge victorious from the Camp Camp Gay Gaymes. Unfortunately, when the Dildo Joust degenerated into hand-to-hand dildo combat, our champion David proved no match for the lipstick lesbian from the Bronx. After the judges declared at the end of the evening that Walt Whitman had won, Kerry, James, Steve, and I stared dejectedly at our feet, unsure of our course in life now that we were losers. Then Kerry proposed a panty raid on the women in Martina Navratilova.

We snuck up to the cabin like gay white ninjas, able by some miracle to keep from giggling, and then James leapt up and took two quick photographs through the window. The women in Martina screamed and we ran in, prancing around and shrieking, "Panty raid! Panty raid!" Cheryl said, "No, guys, for a panty raid you're supposed to *take* panties, not *bring* them." She and Sue, who had gotten engaged the night before, put on matching pairs of funny cardboard glasses and James took more pictures. Sue grabbed the camera and photographed us boys as we posed, smirking, behind the neon sign they had put up that said GIRLS RULE! James looked at the sign, curled his lip disdainfully, and said, "But we don't really believe that." I replied, "We totally do," and we all dissolved into laughter.

It wasn't that this repartee was incomparably witty. But our expansive mood made everything seem funnier and funnier, until we could barely breathe and I fell down. Michael from Oscar Wilde stopped by the cabin. "Okay," he said, "Joel is crawling on the floor. That can't be a good sign." The girls invited us to have a sleepover. Eden explained their nightly rituals. "First we talk about our highs and lows of the day, and then we do guided masturbation." I had not laughed this hard in years. Char added, "We begin by saying, take your left hand *or your right.*" We tried not to be noisy, since it was officially Quiet Time—a stricture imposed upon all of us because Ru-Paul had been keeping the surrounding cabins up till all hours of the night with its partying—but the giddiness bubbling up in us refused to be tamped down.

And the next morning a curious thing happened: at breakfast, my chest wasn't tight. I still felt frightened and alone— these feelings are as much a part of me as my kidneys—but after the panty raid I felt that I belonged somewhere, so feeling frightened and alone was bearable. The people I was eating with had not been involved in the panty raid, yet I felt a kinship with them all the same; I felt connected to them because I felt connected to *someone.* When I saw some cool people sitting at a different table I did not have the impulse to leap up from my seat and attach myself to them, because I did not fear that my only other choice was the horror of being in the middle of a crowd alone with myself. I was content as I was, where I was. It was a strange sensation.

One evening near the end of Camp, Bill Cole announced that the next night would be movie night and that we had three candidates from among which to choose: *Queer Duck, Grease,* and *All About Eve. All About Eve* lost the vote, appallingly, to *Queer Duck;* outraged, three lesbians and I instantly began planning to subvert the stupid will of the stupid majority and steal *Queer Duck* from the office, leaving in its place a copy of *D.E.B.S.,* the 2004 comedy about two teenage lesbian archenemy spies in love. *Queer Duck* was not in the office, however. Apparently it belonged to an individual camper, Joey, so we broke into his cabin, kidnapped the DVD, and left him a note saying it would be returned safe and sound.

We were unable to keep completely silent about our exploit, so it didn't take Michael long to find me the next day to report that Joey was really upset. Joey had been having a difficult time at Camp, said Michael, had felt both friendless and left out, and this violation of his space was the last straw; he had decided to leave Camp the next day.

I spent the afternoon in the art studio breaking sheets of stained glass. Had I really evolved so little since high school? Was I so desperate to be part of the social fabric of a community that I would tread on anybody whose position was more precarious than mine?

All right, we had intended our prank in the spirit of fun, and maybe Joey had reacted more extremely than necessary, but I had considered the possibility that we might hurt him and chosen to disregard it. If the same thing had happened to me my second day here, before the panty raid, how would I not have crumbled? I had entered a society in which I felt I had no place—Bill Cole's speech notwithstanding—and if I had discovered I was being used in a game whose players could have made me happy by talking to me for five minutes, I don't know that I would have decided to leave Camp, but I certainly would have had to work very hard not to cry.

I apologized to Joey and gave him back *Queer Duck,* and he stayed at Camp; Bill ended up screening *But I'm a Cheerleader,* a comedy about a girl whose parents send her to an ex-gay camp, where she becomes a lesbian. Joey wrote me a nice note that ended, "Next time, involve me in what you're planning, and I'll gladly go along."

Next time, involve me in what you're planning. How had I gone so easily from feeling excluded to doing the excluding? Did I dislike the reminder that I hadn't always been on the inside looking out? Was I so relieved to be there that I didn't notice the people who still wanted desperately to be invited in? Had I learned that the only way to be part of a society was to shun its outcasts?

I wrote my high school valedictory speech at four in the morning on the day of my graduation, an event I almost missed because we couldn't figure out how to get my mother's wheelchair down our front steps. "Last night I went to the best party I've ever been to in my entire life," my speech began, and it was true. Matthew Gibson had thrown another party and I had gone to this one and I still didn't belong but since we were all about to escape we were united in the knowledge that, no matter where we belonged, it wasn't *here*. My speech the next day was about how our class would make a difference in the world not because we were particularly smart or kind or wise but because we knew how to have fun. I quoted Hesse and *Auntie Mame;* I closed with the first Dorothy Parker poem I had ever encountered, at age eleven, written in my mother's careful script on the frontispiece of her tattered high school copy of Castarède's *Complete Treatise on the Conjugation of French Verbs.* I looked out at my fellow graduates as I read the opening lines

of "Observation," in praise of good behavior, and smiled as I
continued reading, cataloguing the felicities of a life lived vir-
tuously. "But I shall stay the way I am," Dorothy and I finished,
"Because I do not give a damn."
This was not the speech that I, bookish and abstruse, had
been expected to make. I heard later that the school priest had
called it shameful, but his name was Chaplain Lent, so it was
hard to take him seriously. In my farewell I did not play the role
I had allowed myself to be assigned; I was no longer the outsider peering forlornly through the window. Instead, I turned
my back on a community that had never known how to welcome me and left in search of one that would. And as I glanced
over my shoulder, I felt for the first time that in fact my classmates were the ones behind the gate, and that I had the wide
world before me. In my heart of hearts I knew also that,
though the network of older gay men and women that had sustained me through high school—and, more importantly, introduced me to *The Women*—had probably saved my life, my true
place was no more with them than it was with my classmates.
It was somewhere Out There, and I was On My Way.

But that was fifteen years ago, and what I believe now is
that no one really belongs anywhere. People aren't tidy cre-
ations to be stacked neatly in the Tupperware or poured in pre-
measured quantities from a box into the Cuisinart with no
spills; everybody alive is a lost and disastrous mess. I may not
have felt that I belonged among my classmates, but neither did
Theo Moore and neither, I am astonished to find myself thinking, did Suzanne Hutchinson. The scattered moments of kinship we feel with others are, when reduced to their most basic
elements, accidental discoveries of kinship with ourselves. And
that, I suspect, is what happened that night in Martina
Navratilova: my laughter grew and grew until it was finally

loud enough for me to follow it to its source, which was the community that fills everybody everywhere.

On the final day of Camp, all two hundred of us gathered to spend an hour doing the Walk of Angels. It took me so long to bubble-wrap the fabulous purple-and-green stained-glass tulip window I had finally finished that I worried I would miss Camp's last official activity, but I came running up to the group just as Bill started explaining the rules. We stood in two lines facing one another a few feet apart. As Campers from the heads of the lines walked slowly one by one down the middle, eyes shut, arms folded across the chest, the people standing on either side reached out to guide them, until they got to the end safely and rejoined the lines.

As the first person came down the line toward me, I touched her shoulder tentatively. Hunky David, next in line, touched her arm with one hand and cradled her head briefly with the other. I instantly began using this gesture for the next several Campers but then I worried that if David saw that I'd stolen his idea he would stop liking me so I went back to the tentative shoulder touching.

And they kept coming, men, women, timid, bold, tall, short, in between. Some people wept as they walked; others smiled almost beatifically; still others wore expressions that de-fied classification but that were clearly woven from a deep inner peace. And in the moment of contact I communed with every one of them, protecting them in concert with a host of others. When Joey passed me I gave his shoulder a little squeeze. His eyes were closed so he couldn't see it was me but perhaps he knew anyway. Perhaps he didn't feel the need to know.

Then it was my turn to take the walk. Just before I started, Char—the grandmother who stood before the head of the line—hugged me and whispered in my ear, "Safe journey, angel," just as she had whispered, she told me later, to each Camper who passed. I closed my eyes and remembered her laughing during the panty raid and began the walk.

And with my eyes shut, it was impossible to tell whether any given person reaching for me was cool or a misfit, impossible to long for approval or for distance. All I could do was accept the grace flowing from each hand that touched me. I had planned to smile almost beatifically as I walked but I forgot, so I ended up with an expression that defied classification but that was clearly woven from a deep inner peace.

The strangest thing about the walk was that it seemed to go on forever. The two lines were each only a hundred people long, but as I walked farther and farther the hands I felt became the hands not just of the people around me but of everyone I had ever known, of Mark and Suzanne and Julie and Stacey and Kathy and Chaplain Lent and Luke and Chip and even people I had never met, Bianca who was hot sex in a bottle and her bunkmates Ashley and Jenny and Emily and Bill Cole's father's friend beaten to death with a baseball bat and Martina Navratilova and Barney Frank and Dorothy Parker and Castarède and Oscar Wilde and Walt Whitman and Hesse and Auntie Mame; they were all reaching for me, and infinity was in the palms of their hands, and I thought I held eternity in that hour. And every time I thought I was coming to the end one of them grasped my arm or my head or my back and together we took another step forward.

ON DATING

*In the last month I have gone on dates with nine different
men. They have all been either cute and smart but not funny,
cute and funny but not smart, or funny and smart but not
cute. Or cute and smart and funny but not attracted to me.
Those are the ones I hate the most. My unfavorite quote from
an e-mail: "i should admit that my attraction to you is
purely platonic, but that needn't hinder us from pursuing a
friendship, if that is not outside your agenda." Outside my
agenda, indeed. I hate you and will laugh and laugh when
you arrive in the special circle of hell reserved for people who
don't capitalize the first-person singular pronoun. Ha, ha,
ha. That's me laughing.*

—*The Search for Love in Manhattan*, 8:07 a.m., February 10, 2002*

One day shortly after Tom and I broke up, my friend Rob
and I were eating lunch at Café 82, discussing my apparently

---

*I saw the author of this e-mail three years later at a Margaret Cho concert
and he looked *terrible*. He hadn't gotten fat, but his face was lined and haggard

doomed search for my soul mate, and I realized that a handsome man sitting alone at a nearby table was staring at us. Except that Rob was facing away from him, so it was very possible that he was staring at *me*. I mentioned this to Rob, and we spent the rest of lunch deep in conjecture about the handsome man's motives. After we left the restaurant, I hemmed and hawed on the sidewalk outside for five minutes and then ran back in, wrote my name and phone number on the handsome man's napkin, and fled before he could tell me he had been looking at me because I had a bug in my hair.

A few hours later, after I had gotten home, he called and asked whether I wanted to go out with him that evening. We met outside his apartment; as we walked, he asked me what I'd thought of the State of the Union address a couple weeks before, and I told him that I hadn't seen it because I was depressed enough by the state of the union without having to watch the president lie about it. He said he'd seen it on CNN and asked what TV I watched and I told him *Alias* and *Buffy the Vampire Slayer* and I could actually see him deciding that I was a moron. He kept talking and talking about news media and I wanted to interrupt him and say, *Excuse me, I graduated summma cum laude from Harvard, so why don't you just shut the fuck up?* but I thought that if I did he might not love me so instead I kept quiet.

He led us to a bar where there was a dance party in full swing. I'm not sure how we got in, since the bouncers were clearly under orders not to allow anyone to walk through the

---

and droopy enough to suggest years spent wandering the desert in search of the Promised Land. Far be it from me to suggest that he had the Promised Land within his grasp and that his present desiccation was merely the natural result of his failure to do anything about it when he had the chance.

door who was capable of growing facial hair, but there we were, shrieking in each other's ears and looking ghastly under the unflattering neon lights. At one point I tried to get a little familiar and he demurred, explaining that this was not a date—perhaps he believed I had given him my number because I longed to hear his thoughts about Frida Kahlo?—and then he exchanged e-mail addresses with two other guys in the bar. He spent the entire cab ride back to his place alternately tweaking my nipples and squeezing my crotch, before refusing to invite me into his apartment because it was a mess.

After I regaled Rob and his boyfriend David with the tale of this latest in the string of awful dates through which I had recently suffered, Rob said, "You should start a blog for all these stories."

"What's a blog?" I asked.

"It's like an online diary."

I was dubious. "What if people found it and hated me for writing about them?"

"Just use initials instead of people's names," suggested David. "But not their real initials."

"What would I call it?"

"*The Search for Love in Manhattan,*" said Rob.

"Or *I Hate Everyone I Go on a Date With,*" offered David.

"Potato, potahto," I said.

> *My ex-boyfriend M.T., who moved out in December, came over tonight to play with our dog A. She danced around him with uncontrollable joy at seeing him again and then peed on the floor.*
>
> *I wish I could believe that this wasn't in some way a metaphor for my life.*

—*The Search for Love in Manhattan,* 11:35 p.m., February 13, 2002

Tom and I started out as a terrific couple. On our second date, buying snacks before watching our movie rental, we had the following exchange:

> TOM: How about these salt-and-vinegar potato chips?
> JOEL (*his voice full of wonder*): Oh, my *God*, I *love* salt-and-vinegar potato chips!
> TOM (*his voice also full of wonder*): Really? *Me too!*

and I knew I had found The One. This was very convenient, as Tom lived four blocks away from me, which, given the lake of fire that is the New York public transportation system, is more than reason enough to date anybody; his being handsome and talented was just icing on the cake.

"I've never felt this good in a relationship," I told Rob.

"But you've never been *in* a relationship," he responded.

"You are a bad person," I said.

Two years later, Tom and I were living in a huge apartment so far north of central Manhattan that no one ever visited us. We painted the front hall with a faux finish so it looked like sandstone blocks from an Egyptian pyramid; we bought an aquarium coffee table and brightly colored fish to swim around in it; we made each other profoundly unhappy. We had moved in together despite both being bottoms and both wanting to be the one who got taken care of. We never fought. Instead, when we disagreed about anything, we started crying, and whoever cried harder won. We dealt with everything this way: our sexual incompatibility, our finances, our bathroom towels (I had to cry particularly hard to win that one, but in the end all my friends agreed with me that the purple towels looked much better than blue ones would have). Neither of us had a job to speak of, with the exception of Tom's brief stint as a dog walker that paid almost nothing and cracked the skin on the soles of his feet so severely that they bled. I became increasingly controlling and he became increasingly helpless until finally we were more parent and child than anything else. He cheated, I watched *The Golden Girls* all day and got fat, and when he broke up with me he tricked me into keeping the dog even though I told him I wanted never to be responsible for another living thing again. Luckily, she has turned out to be the light of my life, so I figure I came out ahead in that one.

> *Last night I was at E.S.'s apartment and we were making out and all I wanted was to get the sex over with so that we could eat the cookie dough I'd brought.*
> *I worry that my priorities are misplaced.*
>
> —*The Search for Love in Manhattan,* 6:03 p.m., March 2, 2002

At first the only people who read my blog were friends to whom I sent the Web address. But then I learned that if I went to other people's blogs and left comments, they would come to *my* blog, and sometimes they would link to it from *their* blogs, which would in turn direct their readers to me, or at least those among their readers who had taste. The instant I realized this I became a shameless sycophant, leaving unctuous comments on every blog I visited, even the ones I loathed because their authors misused apostrophes or were more attractive than me. More people started reading my blog, and even more people started reading it when I started writing about all the casual sex I was having in between dates. I was glad I had decided to post under a pen name—a play on the name of the eponymous hero of Marlowe's *Tragedie of Doctor Faustus,* about a learned man who sells his soul to the devil for a stick of gum—because Faustus, M.D., was able to write all sorts of things about the

men I was going out with that I could never have allowed myself to say.

I blogged about L., for example, whom I adored before I
met him because his online profile used the word "trend-
mongering" and referred favorably to television psychic Miss
Cleo. His e-mails were charming and funny and had the
panache that I knew would be the hallmark of my future husband's every communication. Then I met him and he was so
prissy I wanted to shove him into the Hudson River. "I don't
think anyone has felt such disappointment," I wrote, "since
Madame Curie realized that radium wasn't all fun and games."

I blogged about the above-mentioned E.S., with whom I
ate cookie dough and had spectacular sex but who ruined
everything one morning by calling me his boyfriend. I shut
my eyes, hoping that he would vanish into thin air while I
wasn't looking, but when I opened them again he was still
there, so I gave him a sickly smile and pretended I hadn't noticed. I worried that he would figure out I was actually sleeping
with every third man in Manhattan (and every fifth man in
Queens), and, indeed, after one particularly active weekend,
he got a funny look on his face when he saw how far the pile
of condoms in my drawer had dwindled, but luckily I was
able to distract him by baking him a strawberry-rhubarb pie.
E.S. was cute and funny and smart but ultimately kind of boring and therefore ineligible to be my soul mate. I realized that
the reason I kept telling him the same stories over and over
again was that I had nothing else to say to him, so I added
"stimulating" to the "cute, smart, and funny" checklist and
kept looking. I didn't mention any of this to E.S., as I didn't
want to hurt his feelings or cut off my access to the spectacular sex.

I blogged about K.T., with whom I had a fabulous lunch

date and who then revealed that he was a sex addict. It was unclear to me whether he wanted to date me or not, but I gushed on my blog about how not only was he handsome but he also knew when to use the three-period ellipsis and when to use the four-period ellipsis and about how his failure to ask me for my hand in marriage on the spot obviously meant that no one would ever love me. I left out the part about his being a sex addict because I was ashamed that he was *hooked* on the stuff and *still* didn't go to bed with me. In the end it turned out that he did not want to date me, although that was okay, as by the time he told me this he had gained twenty pounds, every one of which he wore badly.

> *This afternoon I went on a date with a guy I met through planetout.com. He sent me a charming e-mail that contained no grammatical errors, so I had high hopes. The first several minutes went well; he was cute and smart and possibly funny (I couldn't quite tell but there were promising glimmers). Then he mispronounced the word "cache."*
>
> *I wish I could let it not matter. But I also wish I had telekinetic powers and were best friends with Queen Noor of Jordan, and I don't seem to have gotten very far with those. I left as soon as I could.*

—*The Search for Love in Manhattan,* 12:47 a.m., June 10, 2002

What is wrong with these men? I asked the universe silently. All I wanted was somebody who was gorgeous, hysterically funny, a towering genius, a master of sparkling repartee, fabulously wealthy, blond, multilingual (my dream was that he would speak eight languages but I was willing to settle for five, as long as he could punctuate correctly in all of them), and possessed of beautifully shaped teeth. I wouldn't even have to trick him into thinking that I was just as perfect as he was, because simply being with him would wipe out my faults as utterly as if they were the city of Carthage or Jennifer Grey's old nose. Was that so much to ask?

It is easy to see in retrospect that what I longed for was not a boyfriend but a version of me without my defects—a man in whom I could see myself as flawless, a man whose jokes always caused riotous laughter instead of sometimes falling flat, whose German was fluent instead of passable, who actually knew everything instead of pretending to and then Googling it when he got home. He would make no mistakes and he would not hate himself.

But at the time none of this was apparent to me; all I knew was that everyone I went out with was catastrophically deficient in some fundamental way—his personality, his politics, his shoes. I began to think that the man I was looking for didn't exist.

And then I met H.N.

Tonight I have a date with a fellow named H.N., who got in touch with me after reading my blog. We have been IMing over the last few days and I have been so charmed and delighted that I know I am in real trouble. We discussed the fact that we were trying to manage our expectations of each other and failing miserably. He gallantly volunteered not to bathe for two days before our first meeting, so as to put some disappointment into the mix right from the beginning; I said in turn that I would pick my nose and be rude to the waitstaff. Still, even with those controls in place, I'm not sure either of us will be able to handle realizing that the other is actually mortal.

The reason I am able to blog about him now is that he

volunteered to stop reading my blog because, he said, he didn't want me to have to censor myself.

Who could not love this man? I mean, to deny himself what must surely be one of the greatest joys available to humankind—reading my pathetically neurotic account of my pathetically neurotic life—so as to allow me to express myself freely—that's true kindness.

He did misspell doppelgänger twice, but the second time was clearly a typo (perfectly acceptable when you're IMing)* and did not contain the mistake he'd made the first time, so it's clear that he actually knows how the word is spelled.

—*The Search for Love in Manhattan,* 5:58 p.m., June 25, 2002

H.N. was not fabulously wealthy, octolingual, or blond, but he was gorgeous and funny and skilled enough in the art of repartee to allow me to put these oversights down to a caprice of fate. We met at Tea & Sympathy, my favorite restaurant in New York, and I enjoyed myself utterly, something that hadn't happened on a date in a long time. Our conversation ranged far and wide, touching on passion, family, our childhoods.

"My parents knew I was gay when they told me I didn't have to go to school the day *Return of the Jedi* opened and I went anyway," he said.

"How did that tip them off?" I asked.

"I went because I didn't want to miss choir practice."

· After dinner we walked up Broadway, as easy in conversation as if we'd known each other for years. When he mentioned being frustrated because he'd finished that week's *New York Times* Sunday crossword puzzle in a day and wouldn't have

---

*This is a lie. Typos are a sign of a deeply flawed character. But I was deceiving myself too.

anything to occupy his free time during the week, it was all I could do not to rip his clothes off and ravish him right there on Seventeenth Street. I settled for grabbing him and kissing him and hoping that he could tell from my erection that I was giving him an IOU.

By exercising a Cistercian monastery's worth of willpower, we managed to get to the end of our first date without undressing. At the end of our second date, however, we recognized that the repetition of such a feat would be impossible, so we went back to my place and resolved the last uncertainty—the question of his prowess in bed—by having terrific sex. Soon afterward I finally dumped E.S., he of the cookie dough and the strawberry-rhubarb pie (though I neglected to finish the second sock of the pair I was knitting him before he moved to Boston, which protracted the unpleasant process of dumping him, but his feet were really big, so I couldn't go any faster); H.N. and I were obviously destined for each other, and all that remained was for us to pick out a china pattern.

Except that as I continued to see H.N. over the next several weeks, going to the Marriott Marquis with him to make out in the elevators, sharing raspberry chocolates with him on his lunch break, cuddling with him on the couch during *The Golden Girls,* the faintest sense of doubt began to suffuse my thoughts about him. He punctuated beautifully and in his presence my faults melted away. When I freaked out because the power had gone off in my apartment, before my computer battery ran out he IMed me, "I wish I were there so I could make you feel a little bit safe, a little bit protected."

And yet, every once in a while, when he was talking about his stupid, incompetent coworker, I caught a hint of something that made me feel uncomfortable. I do not wish to be misunderstood: I detest the stupid and incompetent just as much as the next misanthrope, if not more. But his mockery of her seemed to have a mean-spirited edge. When he talked about her I said nothing and felt ashamed.

I began to notice this edge more and more in his conversation, but I ignored it since he was perfect in all other ways. I made lists of different places we might end up living; I wrote draft after draft of our answering-machine message ("Hi, you've reached H.N. and Joel"/"Hello, this is Joel and H.N."/ "This is the dog; H.N. and Joel can't come to the phone right now"). Then he broke up with me.

"I find myself being more drawn to this new person," his e-mail said, "and well, I kind of want to see what might happen with it. . . . I hope we can still stay in touch with each other, and somewhere down the line grab smoothies and chuckle over 'that crazy summer.' " His misspelling of "consistent" and "reunited" elsewhere in the message was cold comfort.

With the help of my brother's girlfriend I drafted a tortuous response filled with lines like, "I was beginning to feel the same way too" and "There always was something that wasn't quite working, wasn't there?" My brother took one look at my computer screen and snorted in disgust. "You can't send that," he said. "Just write him back and say, fine."

My brother's girlfriend and I stared agog at the audacity of this suggestion, and then I wrote the following e-mail:

> Dear H.N.,
> Okay. I figured as much.
> Joel

I sent it (when I forwarded it to my friend Rachel she wrote back, "ooh, you gave so little!") and swore I would not go on another date for a year. This vow lasted a week and a half, at which point I added "compassionate" to the checklist, decided for good measure not to answer any online ads with less than impeccable orthography and grammar, and went once more unto the breach.

A week ago my friend D.R. and I spent the evening at Drip, a café that sells delicious Oreo milk shakes and has three-ring binders full of personal ads. There are four binders of Men 4 Men ads, in whose pages I have found exactly one ad to which I want to reply. But in order to reply to an ad, you have to leave one yourself. So D.R. and I sat there, trying to compose an ad for me based on what we thought this one guy (about whom we knew nothing except what he had put in his ad) would like.

The thing is, his ad is extraordinary. It has taken us three visits to Drip to write me an ad worthy of this guy's.

By the end of the last go-round, we'd come up with answers to all the questions except "looking for." Everything we thought of was either inferior to his answer or already in my ad somewhere else.

So we decided to buy a Middle Egyptian textbook and answer in hieroglyphs.

I have spent the last two hours poring over An Egyptian Grammar *figuring out how to say "somebody who's cute, smart, funny, compassionate, stimulating, and a top" in Middle Egyptian.*

Now I just have to practice drawing the damn things so it doesn't look as if they were done by a developmentally disabled child.

The Middle Egyptian is, as far as I can tell, grammatically correct, though probably stylistically and idiomatically atrocious. A literal translation would read "a beautiful, clever man; he brings me amusement; he cries out for justice; he causes my spirit to rejoice."

"And a top" will have to be in English. I'm sure the Egyptians did that sort of thing, but they don't seem to have carved it on their funerary architecture.

—*The Search for Love in Manhattan*, 1:45 a.m., September 30, 2002

I quote my ad here:

—*The Search for Love in Manhattan*,* 7:31 a.m., October 23, 2002 †

---

* I recently started studying Middle Egyptian in earnest, and it is now clear to me that the reason the extraordinary-Drip-ad guy never responded to my ad was that the Middle Egyptian was *complete gibberish*. Here is what I should have written:

(Loosely translated, "a man beautiful of form, excellent of mind, effective at causing laughter, who came forth from the womb open-hearted to the suffering and afflicted, and who is master of the secrets of jubilation." After last week's homework I can also add "who knows how to reattach a severed head" but I worry about limiting the applicant pool. I still can't say "and a top," but I'm only on Lesson 14, so the relevant vocabulary may be coming up.

† I am including this pair of blog posts and the previous footnote only so as to be able to drop casually the fact that I know Middle Egyptian. Please love me?

Some of the things I most enjoy doing in bed are jokingly associated with timidity, passivity, and weakness. Since I am timid, passive, and weak, however, I have no problem with this. I spend most of my waking moments shoring up my emotional defenses so as to make myself untouchable. I am an expert at forcing people to talk to me about their problems without revealing any of my own; I am so helpful to others that I leave no room for others to help me. However, I realize that even I cannot be continuously vigilant, so I have decided that the one time I will let myself be vulnerable is during sex.

Depending on shape, size, and technique, the physical experience of coitus isn't always the most comfortable. When I have sex I am opening myself up to the possibility of feeling pain, something I never do otherwise, ever. But I always feel that my partner is keeping me inviolably safe, that he is not just taking care with my physical well-being but keeping watch over the truth of who I am, that for these few moments I can loose my pinions and be infinite, because there exists someone in the world who won't let anything bad happen to me if I do. Out of bed, I pretend that I need no one and nothing. But unclothed and coupled, protected only by trust and a Trojan, I can admit that I am not an island and that, thank God, I never will be.

I suppose I could have written that in the Drip ad, but "and a top" took up much less room.*

---

* Extraordinary-Drip-Ad Guy, I've corrected my Egyptian mistake. Why haven't you called yet? That's okay, e-mail is better, anyway. My computer is set to check it every minute, so when you get in touch I'll be able to write back immediately.

*Those of you who've been reading my blog since the
beginning, as well as those of you who have joined late in the
game but who have read back through the archives, may
remember E.S., a man whom I dated for several months before
breaking up with him. He thought we were something serious
and I thought we were something casual—so casual, in fact,
that, while dating him, I slept with a third of Manhattan,
singly and in groups, and blogged about it all.*

—*The Search for Love in Manhattan,* 9:31 p.m., November 17, 2003

E.S. was one of those weird people who stay friends with
their exes rather than hoping they get stranded on desert is-
lands with just enough food and water to be lonely forever, so
even after I broke up with him I still saw him, platonically,
when he was in town. Every once in a while I'd think, *Gee,
maybe I made a mistake breaking up with him—he's a great guy and I
have lots of fun hanging out with him,* but I'd always end up deciding no, I'd done the right thing.

Soon after he moved back to New York we made the terrible mistake of going to see *Underworld,* which I had expected
to be bad but not nearly as bad as it was. Furthermore, it was
Yom Kippur, the Jewish Day of Atonement, on which we
traditionally fast from one sundown to the next, so I had to
watch the damn thing without any candy to distract me from
its insipidity.

After the movie, we wandered around Union Square, talking about nothing in particular and having a good time. Eventually I started getting cold, so I turned toward the subway,
but then he said, "Actually, let's sit down for a while, because
there's something I want to talk to you about."

There is absolutely nothing that strikes more terror into
my heart than hearing the last nine words of that sentence. So

I sat down, quivering now both from the cold and in anticipatory dread of whatever awful thing he was going to force me to discuss.

As it happened, I wasn't quivering nearly enough, because what he said was, "I read your blog. All of it."

I felt an immediate impulse to leap into the path of oncoming traffic in the hope that there was a Mack truck very close by. Paralyzed by cold and horror and guilt and shame and my desire to disintegrate, however, my body refused to act on this impulse, and so instead I sat there in silence, staring at my lap because I was about as capable of looking E.S. in the face as I was of flying to the moon. I'm sure only a minute or two went by, but it seemed to me as if I remained mute for the length of the entire Cretaceous Period plus half the Tertiary Period before I spoke.

"I'm trying to figure out what to say that won't be meaningless," I said.

"Just say the truth," he said. So I did.

And what followed was an extraordinary conversation about honesty and letting others in and fear and facing your emotions and telling people what you really think. None of these things has ever been my forte. My standard modus operandi is to tell people what I think they want to hear so that they won't find out who I really am and despise me. But in this case there was no escape route open. I had to talk about how I actually felt, which was a confusing mix of ambivalent, cavalier, and affectionate. I said things like, "I had fun hanging out with you but I didn't ever think we were going to be boyfriends" and "That time I was late meeting you for dinner was because I had been having sex with somebody else," and he said things like, "It hurts to hear that but I'm glad you're being open with me" and "Did you really think I didn't know that?"

And it was wonderful.

It turned out that, about a month earlier, he'd seen somebody's online profile that contained a link to that person's blog, which linked in turn to mine. E.S. realized it was me after two seconds—so much for Faustus's attempt at anonymity—and went back to read the archived entries from the time we were dating.

"I understand why you did what you did," he said. "You were just out of a serious relationship, you should have had 'rebound' stamped on your forehead. What upset me was that you didn't tell me what was going on. I didn't have informed consent."

Finally, the cold made it impossible for us to continue the conversation, so we headed toward the subway. "At first I was furious," he said. "I thought about starting a blog called *Faustus Lies*. But now I feel like the whole thing is actually pretty funny."

"Give me a month to get there," I said. "Right now I want to go home and throw myself out of my window."

"Don't do that. You live on the second floor. You'll just hurt yourself."

And when I woke the next morning, I was still buoyed up by the unwonted freedom of having been honest in a difficult situation for once in my life. And then, remembering that it was still the Day of Atonement, I started thinking, Wait, what if it wasn't *him* who was the problem when we were going out?

What if it was me?

Could it be that my refusal to let him in or show him any real part of myself or see any real part of him had something to do with why I had felt it wasn't working?

He did, after all, fit most of my requirements: he was handsome, smart, funny, compassionate, and a top. What if he was stimulating too and I just hadn't noticed? Furthermore, not only was he a medical student and a gifted painter, but he had at one point in his life actually *hung drywall.* I have never even touched drywall, for fear that I might die or get dust on my clothes.

In the weeks following our Yom Kippur conversation, we spent more time together than we ever had when we were dating—he said he felt a lot better having gotten things off his chest—and I found myself wanting more and more to try again, if he'd even remotely consider such a thing, that is, given the cad I'd turned out to be the first time around.

Eventually I realized that the only thing to do was to ask him. I was prepared for unequivocal rejection—what sane person, after all, would stick his finger in that pencil sharpener again?—but held out a slim hope that he might not be sane.

So we went to another movie (this time it was *Runaway Jury,* the quality of which augured far better for the subsequent conversation than *Underworld* had) and then to dinner at Burritovilla. I ate my chips and salsa and tacos in a fugue state, wanting at every moment to speak but unable to do so. *If I can just say one word,* I thought, *I will have committed myself and I can finish.* So finally I choked out, "There's," thereby committing myself, and followed it with "something I want to talk to you about."

"Okay," he said.

The silence that followed this exchange lasted not for periods but for eras. Staring at the table, because once again I couldn't look him in the face, I kept beginning. "I . . . I wa—. . . I . . ."

And finally, hidden somewhere in the Cimmerian depths of my psyche, I found a store of courage previously unknown to me, screwed it to the sticking place, and said, "I want to ask you out on a date."

He looked at me briefly and said, "Let's go for a walk."

It is difficult to walk while trying at the same time not to explode in flames, but somehow I managed. Eventually he said, "I like you. And I'm really attracted to you. But . . . what's going to be different this time?"

I started speaking, stammering even more than I usually do when I'm nervous. I talked about the powerful effect our conversation on Yom Kippur had had on me; I talked about coming to see him in a new light; I talked about my understanding of what a blackguard I'd been. "I'm a different person than I was a year ago," I said.

"Okay," he said.

"I mean, you can think about it, you don't have to give me an answer now, or if your answer's no I completely understand and—"

"No, I mean, okay, I'll go out on a date with you."

Then I burst into tears.

Which was the first time I'd done that in front of him, despite having dated him for nine months. So I was already doing better on the emotional honesty front, as I have the urge to burst into tears at least twelve times every day but I always bottle it up. A couple nights later we went to dinner at a Thai restaurant in Brooklyn and I spent the whole evening in agony because the umbilical hernia left over from when I was fat opened up and started letting my intestines out through my belly button. Since I couldn't walk, we took a cab back to E.S.'s apartment, where he manually reduced the hernia—that's really what it's called—and we've been together ever since. He stopped reading my blog long ago.

For Valentine's Day, I baked E.S. an apple pie. He said it was the best apple pie he'd ever had, including all the apple pies I'd baked him before. He said it was perfect. I was quite pleased with this praise, as he is never so effusive unless he really means it.

But two days ago, as we were bringing the now-empty pie plate back to my apartment, we had the following conversation:

FAUSTUS: *I need to find a smaller pie plate. The piecrust recipe I use doesn't generate enough dough to fill this one comfortably.*

E.S.: *Yeah, the crust on that pie was a little bit thin.*

FAUSTUS: *I thought you said it was the best apple pie you'd ever had.*

E.S.: *It was.*

FAUSTUS: *But when you said it was perfect you were lying.*

E.S.: *No, I wasn't! It was perfect!*

FAUSTUS: *Except for the tissue-thin crust, which you hated.*

E.S.: *Look, there's going to be a flaw in any pie.*

FAUSTUS: *Oh, so I'm incapable of making edible pastry.*

E.S.: *It was perfect. But I think of perfection in human terms,*

FAUSTUS: *Why on earth would you do such a ridiculous thing?*

E.S.: *Are you going to be like this forever?*

FAUSTUS: *Yes.*

—*The Search for Love in Manhattan*, 8:26 a.m., February 26, 2005

E.S.'s real name is Mike. He does not speak eight languages, or even five. His conversation is more taciturn than sparkling. He misspells words and mispunctuates sentences. He is losing his hair and when I am with him my faults do not disappear; they are often in fact grotesquely magnified. His teeth are crooked and no whiter than anybody else's. He is not the man I wanted.

But he is smart and funny and handsome and stimulating and profoundly compassionate and great in bed. He has a stronger sense of empathy than anybody I've ever met. He is a psychiatrist in a hospital where he cares deeply about very sick people who think they are the Emperor of Japan or the sun's sister or a butternut squash. He paints beautiful and complex pictures of my dog. He admires me and my work and finds me handsome and puts up with the fact that I am crazy. He likes me even though I am vengeful and punitive. He is the only man I've ever dated who I didn't want to be when I grew up and I love him very much.

So why is it that I wake up sometimes in the middle of the night paralyzed by doubt, staring out the window until the closest thing to certainty I can find is the fear that I'm settling and that really I should hold out for the polyglot millionaire?

And if I'm on a search for love in Manhattan, then why am I moving to Brooklyn with Mike in two weeks?

Why am I frightened that, if I ever do to him in bed what he usually does to me, I will despise him afterward for allowing me to take care of him rather than the other way around, for abdicating his responsibility as my protector and leaving me undefended and alone?

He is an extraordinary man and even after these paragraphs appear in print he will love me.

And as I go to sleep beside him I pray that when I wake up tomorrow that will still be enough.

On Teaching Aerobics

I would probably never have become a step aerobics instructor if the first step aerobics class I attended had not been taught by my soul mate. John was not only scorchingly hot but also, I discovered by Googlestalking him after I got home, a Doctor of Physics. Oh, and just for fun, fluent in Italian.

Naturally I became a regular at his class. I made prodigious efforts to help him understand that he was my soul mate, including but not limited to spending days drafting an e-mail asking him out and then sending it and then going mad with fear when I didn't hear back from him immediately and finally doing the bravest thing I had ever done in my life, which was calling him and actually *leaving him a message asking him out on a date.* (This might possibly have been a braver thing to do if I hadn't written the message out beforehand because I was going to call when I knew he was teaching, after I had called earlier and he had answered and I had hung up and he had *69ed me and called back and I had pitched my voice a major third higher than usual and affected a Southern accent and apologized for dialing the wrong number.)

The voice mail he left in response to my message did not contain the word "yes."

Due to poor planning on my part, I couldn't go to his next class, and I was leaving town the day after that, which meant it would be weeks before I saw him, and he would think I had stopped coming to his class because I was in love with him and couldn't deal with being rejected, and I would never be able to go to his class again because then I would have to see him and be humiliated. I was about to start vomiting in frustration until I checked his website and saw that he would be subbing for another instructor the next morning. The class was at an appallingly early hour but obviously I had no other choice.

When I ran into John on the gym floor before class, he seemed pleasantly surprised to see me; I pretended to have had no idea he was going to be there, and deceitfully claimed that I had a meeting in the neighborhood and had figured I'd just stop by the gym beforehand. I knew from a mutual friend that John had recently returned from a trip to Italy, so I'd practiced several amusing things to say offhand in Italian once he mentioned that he spoke Italian, but by the time I realized he wasn't going to mention that he spoke Italian I'd already said all the amusing things in English, and I didn't trust myself to improvise, so I told him I had to get a drink of water and ran into the locker room.

Class actually went quite well once it started, and I managed to fix my mouth in the semblance of a smile for most of the hour, though this was made more difficult by my uncertainty about whether my staring at him would come across as appropriately watching the teacher or inappropriately gazing at him in pitiful doomed love.

When John went over to the stereo to change the tape, muttering rhetorically, "What's next?" I said, "Chocolate," a piece of humor for which I think I should receive a great deal of credit given my emotional state at the time.

He stared at me, looking baffled, and said, "What?"

Obviously he hadn't heard me, so I took a deep breath and croaked "Chocolate!" a little louder.

"*What?*"

"CHOCOLATE!" I screamed. He continued to stare at me, and somebody else said, "Abs!" and he turned to her and said, "No, abs is later." Then he put in a new tape and I killed myself.

Unfortunately, John didn't notice, so I had to finish the class. I spent the cooldown period deciding to give up step aerobics in despair, but I knew that I would never actually do it, because sadly I had come to enjoy step aerobics too much.

My problem with most exercise is that, while it engages me physically, it leaves me mentally unfettered, which is never a good thing. I'll lie on the bench or sit on the stationary bike or stand on the treadmill for however long I've committed to doing so (well, for however long I've committed to doing so minus fifteen minutes), and as I grunt conspicuously with each repetition or pretend I'm pedaling as fast as I can or bop my head in time to my iPod while sauntering along there is absolutely nothing for my mind to do but spin around in ever-tightening circles far more agonizing than the torture to which I am subjecting my body. This is the main reason I find step aerobics so appealing: you have to pay really close attention to what you're doing for an hour or so, or else you risk getting the steps wrong and looking like a moron in front of the entire class. And when you're paying really close attention to what you're doing for an hour or so, well, that's an hour or so you can't spend thinking about how if you had just gotten Thad Sapphire the small Valentine's Day basket in your senior year of college instead of the big one with the teddy bear you wouldn't have freaked him out and he would have wanted to date you and now you would be happy.

Since I spend basically all my time thinking about how if I had just gotten Thad Sapphire the small Valentine's Day basket in my senior year of college instead of the big one with the teddy bear I wouldn't have freaked him out and he would have wanted to date me and now I would be happy, I found the opportunity to turn my thoughts elsewhere very appealing. So I started going to other step classes taught by other instructors, and then I started getting to know some of those other instructors (a process rendered less exciting but also less intimidating by their consistent failure to be both Doctors of Physics and fluent in a Romance language), and after I had been stepping for nine or ten months I was talking to one of these instructors after class and he said, "Hey, you should think about teaching," and I froze.

Because what on earth could be sexier than being an aerobics instructor?

An aerobics instructor who had *published a book*?

And who *wrote musicals*?

And who *knew French and Italian and German and ancient Greek* though he'd forgotten most of the first three and all of the last and who *had graduated summa cum laude from Harvard* though he'd barely passed his general exams and who *spent all his time looking up things that nobody else knew anything about so that people would think he was smart and like him the most or at least pretend not to notice how pathetic he was?*

Secretly I believe that most of us have a fixed amount of talent we can distribute as we choose between our minds and our bodies. Some people spread themselves evenly and are sort of smart and creative and sort of in shape. Other people pour all their energy into developing one quality and become expert mathematicians or fashion models, but their complementary facets show a lack of focused attention: nobody admired Einstein for his well-developed quadriceps, and Giselle Bündchen's name is nowhere to be found on the list of luminaries Ban Ki-moon has consulted about the International Compact on Iraq. I would never be a Doctor of Physics, so I understood that the zenith of perfection John had attained was beyond my reach, and I was okay with this, except in August when my therapist was out of town. But if I was both a mental genius and a physical one, if I became not only a composer and writer and polyglot and Harvard honors grad but a composer and writer and polyglot and Harvard honors grad *and aerobics instructor*, then what conclusion could I draw but that my terror of ever making a mistake and leading the cute guy next door with the funky haircut to stop speaking to me was groundless because I am actually *way better than everybody else*?

So I practiced and passed my certification test and started teaching and was bad at it and got better and got better still and picked up gigs at fancier gyms and now I teach eight classes a week, give or take, and sometimes I even have fun doing them.

But none of that is as important as the fact that I can think of myself as an aerobics instructor. Because now, when I step into a subway car afraid of every single person I see, at least I can say to myself, well, you're probably the only one on this train who can render the date in the style of the French Revolutionary calendar *and* bench-press more than his own body weight.

Despite my myriad achievements, however, my self-loathing has unfortunately refused to accept that I am the boss of it, and in fact has discovered an even more pernicious way to gain the upper hand. When I'm teaching, Thad Sapphire and the Valentine's Day basket are usually far from my thoughts, but what replaces them is worse, as illustrated in the following table representing a typical class.

WHAT I SAY IN CLASS

Okay, everybody, repeater to the left!

Give me a reverse turn, straddle, reverse turn off the front!

Over the top and pivot!

Knees to your corners!

Everybody give me an L-step!

Hold the Ls! Knees higher, everybody! The farther you move through your range of motion, the more calories you burn!

Mambos around the world!

One knee!

Repeaters left and right!

WHAT I AM THINKING

I have been teaching this class for a year and a half and there are only three people here. I suck. Really it would be better for everybody if I just quit. I wouldn't have to spend every Saturday morning trying to keep what little sense of self-worth I have from seeping out through my pores along with my sweat, and they wouldn't have to go to a sucky aerobics class. Wait, what's the next combination? What does it start with? Fuck, fuck, fuck. Side lifts? No, not side lifts, not an around-the-world, maybe it's an L-step? I'll cue an L-step. Shit, it's not an L-step. Okay, I'll have them do a holding pattern of L-steps while I figure out what comes next. Why isn't Andrea smiling? She was smiling last week. She hates me. Oh, right, next is the mambos. How could I forget the mambos? By getting old, that's how. Why does Andrea hate me? Is it because I fucked up that cue? Maybe she'll like me again if I compliment her shoes after class. Maybe she'll like me again if I bring her brownies next week. If I complimented her shoes *and* brought her brownies, would she think I was weird? Wait, I can't bring her brownies, this is an aerobics class. Shit, what comes next?

Of course, there are occasions on which this internal monologue is hushed too, and when this happens I tend to long for its return.

Rather than using well-known recordings, the companies that release aerobics CDs usually just get the rights to songs and rerecord them in the appropriate format. This means that, when you buy CDs for an aerobics class, even if you know the standard recordings of songs, you don't really know what these versions will sound like until you hear them. If you are a responsible teacher, you listen to your CDs ahead of time to get a feel for the high points and the more relaxed moments, so that you can adapt your routine to the music coming out of the speakers. If you are me, you don't.

Most of the time this presents no significant difficulties. But one day in a class I was teaching with music I hadn't previewed, the CD moved to the next song and suddenly I began to feel very strongly that I had heard this music before. As I continued to call out the steps, I thought, wait, can this really be a cover of *that* song? And shortly thereafter it became clear that yes, this really could be a cover of that song, which was "Without You."

> *No, I can't forget this evening,*
> *Or your face as you were leaving,*
> *But I guess that's just the way the story goes.*
> *You always smile, but in your eyes your sorrow shows.*
>
> *No, I can't forget tomorrow*
> *When I think of all my sorrow,*
> *When I had you there but then I let you go. . . .*

I can't live if living is without you.
I can't live, I can't give any more.

After about fifteen seconds of trying to teach to the song, I ran over to the stereo, said merrily, "Okay, folks, we're going to the next song because I have totally traumatic associations with this one!" and forwarded the CD to the next track, which was, if memory serves, ABBA's "Dancing Queen."

I'm sure my students thought I'd skipped "Without You" because it was a breakup song, which was fine by me. Because my traumatic associations with the song have to do not with any romantic entanglements but with my mother's miscarriage of the child who would have been my older brother. She told me a story once, when the record player had gone quiet, about leaving her doctor's office after getting the news, waiting in the car while my father went into the pharmacy to get her anti-cramp medication, and turning on the radio just in time to hear the DJ introduce "Without You." I'd noticed that whenever we listened to the song she tended to get a funny look on her face, but this was the only time I ever heard her say why. And now I can never hear "Without You" and not think of my mother there in the turned-off car, mourning her dead child—whom she and my father had been referring to as Junior—and knowing that even if she had more children her diabetes would eventually ravage her body and then kill her in the prime of her life. I can't hear that song without thinking of her blighted hopes and her constant struggle against pain and her childhood lived in fear of a monstrous mother and the magnitude of what she was able to accomplish in the world despite the forces ranged so mercilessly against her.

When I'm wandering the aisles of Rite Aid and "Without

You" comes on the store radio, it's not such a big deal; I can take a moment, get wistful, and then go back to hoping that if I brush my teeth with Rembrandt Plus Toothpaste I will be more popular.

But in front of a room full of type-A twentysomethings, shrieking, "Around the world! Knees higher! I know you can do it! Show those calories you mean it!" I found that hearing anybody sing *You always smile, but in your eyes, your sorrow shows. . . . I can't live if living is without you, I can't live, I can't give any more* was unbearable.

Some months ago, several minutes into a class I was subbing for a fellow instructor, a very awkward middle-aged man in the back of the room stopped exercising and went over to lean against the wall. I checked to make sure he was all right and not having a heart attack, and he said everything was fine, but he stayed by the wall for the rest of the hour. After class was over and everybody else had left, I asked him again whether he was okay.

"I'm scared," he said.

"Of what?" I asked.

"Everything." He looked so forlorn that I put a hand on his shoulder, whereupon he started to cry. I did not know how to respond. This was not a situation that had been covered in my American Fitness and Aerobics Association Primary Group Exercise certification class.

After a few moments he regained control of himself. "I'm

starting a new job next month," he said, "and I'm really worried about it. I'm scared of getting old, I'm scared of losing my boyfriend."

Under ordinary circumstances I am a very good listener, mixing warm affirmation with insightful questions in whatever ratio seems appropriate. But this man might as well have been talking to the Babylonian Sphinx. I longed to be somewhere else, the sands of the Gobi desert with no water, anywhere but here. "I'm trying really hard to live in the moment," he said.

"I haven't lived in the moment since 1999!" I laughed desperately. This did not cure his depression.

Eventually I asked him whether he wanted to try exercising again, just the two of us; he said he did, and I spent fifteen minutes teaching him the most basic routine I could come up with, at which he sucked. He kept getting in his own way, lifting his right knee instead of his left or moving backward instead of forward. Finally he did it right twice through and I said brightly, "Great job I have to go meet my friend for brunch bye!" and fled as if the studio had been in flames. I did not have to go meet my friend for brunch. But I could not bear to look into this man's eyes any longer and see such voracious need, because what if I realized that I was standing in front of a mirror?

It was on a cold Tuesday in January that I taught my first aerobics class in the group home for the severely mentally ill.

I have been fascinated by mental illness ever since I can remember. It would be inaccurate to say that I am dating my boyfriend Mike *because* he is a psychiatrist, but I cannot deny that postcoital small talk about Capgras's syndrome (a neurological disorder that leads people to believe that their family members and pets have been replaced by impostors) is not least among the perquisites of our relationship.

The idea of becoming a group fitness instructor to the insane had taken root in my mind when Mike refused, no matter how piteously I begged him, to smuggle me into the Christmas party for his hospital's psych ward. "Why are you so interested?" he asked.

"Because I would get to see crazy people in their natural habitat!"

"The patients go for a walk outside every day. Why don't you just hang out in the park and wait for them to show up?"

"That would only be seeing them from a distance."

"Maybe you could come and teach them aerobics," he said, and though he was joking I understood at once that he had unwittingly revealed my destiny. I couldn't teach at the hospital, it turned out, because of the insurance risk, but I asked around and found a group home that was interested.

This wasn't just a self-serving idea. The medications that control the most severe illnesses also tend to cause serious weight gain and its attendant health problems, so I would be helping the severely mentally ill avoid diabetes, hypertension, and back fat.

Most importantly, though, I would be able to tell people that I taught aerobics in a lunatic asylum.

There are 297 conditions listed in the fourth edition of the *Diagnostic and Statistical Manual,* the resource psychiatrists use to diagnose mental illness. To me the most disturbing of these are the psychotic disorders. Depression I can handle; anxiety I can handle; Munchausen by proxy I actually get a little kick out of.

But these disorders do not necessarily cut those who suffer them off from reality. A psychotic can hallucinate mocking voices, inhabit imaginary universes, become somebody who died three thousand years ago. I really wish people would stop saying "insanity is doing the same thing over and over again and expecting different results" while raising their eyebrows to underscore the deceptively simple profundity of these words. Because insanity is not doing the same thing over and over again and expecting different results; insanity is thinking you're the Empress of China.

(Unless of course you *are* the Empress of China, in which case insanity is throwing yourself a thirty-million-tael birthday party instead of strengthening the military, so that in the wake of the Boxer Rebellion it's a piece of cake for the Eight-Nation Alliance to seize the Forbidden Palace and send you into exile.)

"Psychosis is a protective measure," Mike told me once. "If you believe you're Rameses II then you don't have to deal with the fact that you're actually really sick and living on the streets and addicted to heroin."

"So your job is to take people who think of themselves as extraordinary and gifted and amazing and force them to see that they're actually crazy homeless junkies?"

"Pretty much."

I get it; I really do. But I still believe that there are ways in which the disease is preferable to the cure. The people whose voices order them to hurt others, or whisper to them that passersby are actually witches trying to kill them, them I can understand medicating. But I would rather die in two months as king of the elves than live for years watching everything I have worked to become go to wrack and ruin.

Because one of the most troubling aspects of psychotic disorders is that, though medicine can slow them down, it seems to be unable to halt their progress. Today's antipsychotic drugs are somewhat less likely than their forebears to induce things like sustained painful muscle spasms and irreversible facial tics, but even with medication the odds are apparently one in three that if you are schizophrenic your mind will sooner or later turn to gruel.

"Would you still love me if I developed schizophrenia?" I asked Mike.

"It's probably too late for you. Schizophrenia usually shows up in men by the early twenties."

"Well, would you still love me if I developed late-onset schizophrenia?"

"We would always be very good friends."

I know patients are seriously ill when Mike calls them cute. "We had the cutest kid come in today," he'll say. "She was an intergalactic supermodel."

"What did she think of Tyra Banks?" I'll say.

"Totally over."

The Dorothea Dix Home for Assisted Living was only a few blocks from where I lived, and when I found the address I immediately began to envy the severely mentally ill for living in a fabulous Victorian High Gothic mansion. The interior decorating scheme, unfortunately, featured not mosaics and girandoles but a great number of linoleum tiles, though their flattening effect was mitigated by the light that streamed in from the wide windows. A large man named Kyle led me downstairs to the activity room, where he pushed the couches to the walls and against the pool table and pointed me to the electric outlet.

People started trickling in as I set up the boom box; by four-thirty, the official start time, I had nine students, six women and three men, facing me in two rows. I asked their names, forgot them at once (except for Doug, who impressed himself upon my memory by drooling on my hand when he shook it (drool being a common side effect of antipsychotic medication)), and started the CD. As we warmed up by marching in place, I told the students to breathe deeply on my count. "Breathe in," I said, lifting my arms, and then "Breathe out," lowering them to my sides.

"Breathe in breathe out?" asked a tall caramel-skinned woman in the back row.

"Yes." I demonstrated a couple more times and then we started.

At Mike's urging I had put together the simplest routine I could think of, but I hadn't gone nearly far enough. These people had trouble moving in time to the music and in the right direction; if I forced them to attempt grapevines, chassés, or mambos I would surely regret it. Thinking quickly, I replaced all the traveling steps in the routine with kicks, knee lifts, and hamstring curls, accompanied by peppy arm movements. We also did some finger and toe exercises, to help forestall diabetic breakdown in blood flow to the extremities.

The severely mentally ill seemed to be having a really good time. Three of them never stopped grinning. One gazed off into the middle distance but a smile played at the corners of his lips. A short woman in the front row started whooping in excitement (whooping is always heartening to an instructor).

After twenty minutes or so, we stopped and took a few

minutes to cool off. "Arms slowly above your head," I said, "and then down."

"Breathe in breathe out," said the tall woman in the back row. It wasn't clear to me whether she was asking if she should breathe in breathe out again along with the arm movements or admonishing me for neglecting to instruct the class to breathe in breathe out.

"Yes. Breathe in, breathe out," I said.

"Breathe in breathe out!" she said again.

"Right!"

"Breathe in breathe out!"

"Breathe in breathe out yes now everybody go sit on the couches." I turned the lights off, put on the cooldown CD I had grabbed on my way out the door, and forwarded it to C.H.H. Parry's setting of Psalm 84. *Those who go through the desolate valley will find it a place of springs,* sang the choir, *for the early rains have covered it with pools of water.* I instructed my students to shut their eyes and imagine pools of water and relax their muscles and let their heads slump down onto their chests and feel the stress of the last week drain from their bodies.

I let the CD track play to its end as my students sat in the dark. "Okay, I'll see you guys next Tuesday!" I chirped, and left.

As I walked home, I tried to figure out how I would frame this story to my friends. I had laughed to them beforehand, "Yeah, I'll be all like, 'I don't care if Napoleon is telling you to hold your arms above your head, I want you to move them in circles!' " But nothing remotely like this had been called for.

It would be simple to say that, having thought of the severely mentally ill as a joke, I had been forced to confront our shared humanity. But that wasn't what was going on. I had already known very well that mental illness doesn't change the fundamental makeup of human character. I had cracked jokes about my students-to-be, yes, but I had done so recognizing, at the back of my mind, that laughter is a powerful defense against the threat posed by the hideous disintegration of personhood. If I can keep at a distance the man walking down the subway car pouring orange soda from a two-liter bottle onto each seat and carefully wiping it up with newspaper, if I can think of him as fodder for humor, then I do not have to ask how the world can be so pitiless as to have allowed one of its children to come to this. All those starving-Ethiopian jokes in the eighties were popular for a reason.

It would also be simple to say that I came away from the experience thinking *There but for the grace of God go I,* but that wouldn't be true either. Partially this is because I recognize that most of the factors contributing to psychosis are absent from my life. Mostly, though, I prefer to believe that God has no grace to give. Because the alternative is that He gives grace capriciously or, even worse, that He plays favorites. Some desolate valleys become places of springs, and others wither until they are sere beyond hope, and if God is the one who chooses which is which then I would rather live in a universe lucky enough to have escaped His notice.

Finally I gave up trying to figure out how to tell the story. My friends would just have to wait.

When Mike came home from the hospital that evening, I told him about the class and about the breathe-in-breathe-out lady and about how I couldn't tell whether she was asking a question or rebuking me.

"Neither one," he said. "She was just having a good time. You were saying it, so she joined in. That's the behavior of a person who's very impaired."

"My explanations were less depressing."

Class the following week unfolded in much the same fashion, but the week after that nobody showed up. *Great,* I thought. *Even insane people don't like my class.* I had unplugged the boom box and was putting my sweater back on when who should walk in but the breathe-in-breathe-out lady? "I'm here to exercise!" she said.

There is little I dislike more than teaching an aerobics class of one. A room full of exercisers creates an almost palpable energy, and it's very easy to draw on that energy to teach. When there's one person there, you have to be just as energetic as you do when there are twenty, but there is no crowd to buoy you up, so you have to generate all the energy yourself. When a single person shows up for a class I'm teaching—thankfully a rare event—he or she invariably says, "Oh, if it's just me, let's not worry about it, I don't want to make you stay," to which my oppressive sense of responsibility forces me to reply, "No, no, if you're here to exercise then we're going to exercise!" Then I make up some cockamamie story about really enjoying teaching one person because it means I don't have to try to teach to different levels of experience simultaneously. Then I remind myself to TiVo whatever I want to watch that night because by the time it starts I will be dead to the world.

But Sarah (such was, I finally learned, the breathe-in-breathe-out lady's name) was here to exercise, and besides I really enjoy teaching one person because it means I don't have to—oh, never mind.

The CD I had brought that day started with a remix of Whitney Houston's "How Will I Know?" "You like Whitney?" Sarah asked as we moved from step-touches to marching in place.

"Yeah," I said. She started giggling. "What? What's so funny?"

"You like Whitney!" She kept giggling.

"Do *you* like Whitney?" I asked, trying to keep the edge out of my voice. I am insecure enough about my taste in popular music without having it impugned by a crazy person.

"Not really."

"Oh, then let me change the song."

"No, I like this song. Breathe in breathe out, right?"

"Right."

We moved into side lunges with reaches. Sarah was an inept exerciser, but what she lacked in skill she made up for in enthusiasm. When the CD moved to the next track and Laura Branigan started singing ("Was it something that he said/Or the voices in your head/Calling Gloria?"), Sarah sang along. "This is good for your muscles, right? Makes you strong?"

"Well, it makes your heart strong. And that makes you healthier."

"Breathe in breathe out," she nodded.

By now Sarah seemed able to handle the basic steps of the routine, so I figured I'd add some variety. "Flap your arms like a chicken," I said, demonstrating and making chicken noises. This is not a standard aerobics move but I secretly enjoy making chicken noises and I was glad to have an excuse. Sarah flapped her arms dutifully, though she did not join me in the chicken noises. "Okay, follow me," I said as the CD moved to the next track. I step-touched forward, still flapping my arms, and led Sarah around the room, out into the hall, and back in again.

I am dancing around a pool table, flapping my arms and clucking like a chicken while the Weather Girls sing "It's Raining Men," I thought, *and **she's** the crazy one?*

"I like you," Sarah said as we started heel digs.

"Oh, thank you," I said, very nervous about where she might be headed.

"*As a person,* I mean," she said quickly. "You understand? I like you *as a person.*"

"I like you too," I said, relieved. "Okay, watch my feet here and do what I'm doing."

For the next few weeks, Sarah was the only person to show up for my class. "I have to stay out of trouble," she said one day during hamstring curls. "Stay away from boys, you know?"

"Boys are definitely a lot of trouble," I said.

"I want to get married, so I have to stay out of trouble."

"Who do you want to get married to?"

"I don't know yet. First I have to get well. You know I'm mentally ill, right?"

"Yes. That's terrific, move your legs exactly like that. You're doing a great job!"

"I want to stay away from boys, stay out of trouble, so I can get married. I was going out with a boy but it was too much so I stopped. Are you going out with anybody?"

"Yeah."

"Do you want to marry her?"

I turned to stone.

During the ensuing silence I continued the knee lifts. "Nah," I said finally.

"Why not?"

"Oh, I don't know. I'm just not the marrying kind. Move your arms like you're throwing a basketball. Yes!"

Swish

But the thing is, I *am* the marrying kind. I want desperately to get married (by which I mean *married* married, not civilly united or domestically partnered or any other modified participial adjective the government might condescend to toss me). Mike and I have spent hours arguing about our theoretical wedding. I want us to get married grandly, wearing morning clothes. I'd book the Basilica di San Marco for the event if I could, but I do not hold out much hope that the Patriarch of Venice His Eminence Angelo Cardinal Scola will be easily won over. Mike, on the other hand, wants to get married in shorts in the middle of the woods. When he revealed this and I asked him, appalled, where our guests would sit, he actually said, "On the beautiful green earth." The fact that I did not break up with him at once should be taken as an indication of how deeply I care for him.

So how could I paint Sarah a picture in which he was nowhere to be found?

Even as I told myself I was protecting her, I knew it wasn't true; I was protecting myself. But from what? Did I think she was going to bash me? The medicated mentally ill are statistically no more violent than the general population. Furthermore, even if she had tried to harm me, she was not physically strong enough to do so, and it would have been the work of three seconds to overpower her. We were in a neighborhood known less for its enlightened acceptance of gay people than for its history of race riots, but that had been years before, and besides Sarah was from somewhere else.

Not long after I had started teaching aerobics, a friend interviewing me for a project in her sociology class asked, "Has discomfort with being open about your sexuality ever led you to modify your behavior?"

"Nope, never," I had answered breezily.

But I realized now that my answer had been a total lie and that in fact I modified my behavior all the time. What about four days earlier, when I had told a waitress at Chevy's in Times Square that my *friend* needed a refill on his soda? What about the week before that, when I had pretended not to hear the teenage punk shout "faggot" at me as I went through the turnstile into the subway? What about the week before that?

"What would you say being gay means to you?" my sociology-student friend had asked.

I had thought for a long time before saying, "It's nothing, and it's everything."

Yes, being gay is just one of a thousand thousand traits that make up my character, no more remarkable than my love of M&M's or my ability to mess up a room in fifteen seconds flat or my failure to understand the appeal of Luke and Owen Wilson.

But I believe that the desire to love and be loved is the strongest force on earth. And in that way, being gay affects every interaction in which I take part—just as being straight affects every interaction in which straight people take part. Every human motive is in the end a yearning for companionship, and every act of every person on this planet is an effort not to be alone.

So what right did I have to sneer at Sarah when I thought she harbored a romantic interest in me?

The following week three people came to class, including Doug, the drooling guy, and the whooper from the first day, whose name, it turned out, was Jane. Sarah, meanwhile, was in a bad mood. "My brother and sister get more rest than me," she said. "I don't think that's fair. Do you think that's fair?"

"Um," I said.

Fifteen minutes into the class, she asked Jane—who had

started whooping again—whether she was tired. "No," said Jane, and kept on aerobicizing. Sarah looked at me and mouthed *she's tired* while making the crazy-screwball gesture with her finger beside her head.

I wondered whether I should report to anybody that Sarah was in a bad mood, but then I figured, hey, it's a group home, they already know.

"I love your hair!" said Jane to me between whoops, without breaking the hamstring-curl pattern. "I used to have hair just like that."

"Oh, thanks!" I said. "But I think you have fabulous hair now." Her hair was actually pretty great, equal parts copper and brass, held straight out from the back of her head with a bandanna. "Terrific work, keep going just like that!" Sarah looked unhappy at being left out of the conversation so I opened my mouth to tell her she was doing terrific work too but what I heard myself say was, "Breathe in breathe out!"

"Breathe in breathe out!" she responded enthusiastically.

For relaxation music at the end of class I had brought a CD of François Couperin's *Lessons for Tenebrae*, a profound lamentation for Jerusalem exiled in Babylon. *The ways of Zion do mourn*, sang the soprano in Latin. *All her gates are desolate, her priests do sigh.*

"Shut your eyes," I said as I turned the lights off. "Listen to the music. Relax your muscles. Let your head slump down onto your chest. Feel the stress of the last week drain from your body." The *Lessons for Tenebrae* are not uplifting, like Psalm 84 with its early rains and pools of water, but the music is more compassionate.

And from the daughter of Zion all her majesty is departed; her princes are become like harts that find no pasture, and they are gone without strength before the pursuer.

Suddenly Jane started singing along, unhindered by the fact that she knew neither the words nor the music. The quality of her voice suggested not mental illness but something like peace.

All that honored her despise her, because they have seen her nakedness: Yea, she sigheth, and turneth backward.

Jane, Sarah, and Doug were all sitting on the couch in the darkened activity room, and I stood next to them. We had a minute or two left before class was officially over. And in the meantime, Doug remained still, and Jane kept singing, and I thought about going through the desolate valley and finding it a place of springs, and Sarah kept breathing in, breathing out, breathing in, breathing out.

ON MUSICAL THEATER

I always thought musicals were stupid.

But I changed my mind during my senior year at Harvard not long after a girl named Gina Grant was admitted for the following autumn. The national media made a huge fuss over her: she had an IQ of 150, she was co-captain of her high school's tennis team, in her spare time she tutored underprivileged children—and all this despite the fact that both of her parents had been dead for years. She became a latter-day Horatio Alger, shining proof that anybody could scale Olympus by working hard enough, even an orphan.

Unfortunately the reason she was an orphan, the media soon discovered, was that at the age of fourteen she had used a lead crystal candlestick to bludgeon her mother to death. She had served six months in a juvenile penitentiary for her crime and her file had been sealed, but Harvard revoked her admission all the same, and in the fall she enrolled at Tufts.

I believed, along with most of my peers, that Harvard had mishandled the situation badly. Not that Gina Grant should have been lauded for her actions, but what right did Harvard have to render its own judgment above and beyond what the state had already deemed appropriate? Horatio Alger was no longer telling this story; he had been replaced by Thomas Hardy. Here was a girl who had made a mistake—an awful one, to be sure—and whose dream had as a result been placed forever out of her reach.

None of this made the story any less funny, though, so of course my family became obsessed with her. Not only because of the Harvard connection, but also because she was from South Carolina, where we lived. I couldn't call home without spending an hour talking about Gina Grant. It was as if we were tuned to our own Gina Grant Channel, all Gina Grant, all the time. One evening my brother, choking with laughter, suggested that I write a musical about her. I thought this was the most hilarious thing I'd ever heard and the next day I shared the joke with all my friends, who also thought it was the most hilarious thing they'd ever heard.

One of these friends was a director, coincidentally also named Gina. "I'm going to write a musical about Gina Grant, hahahahaha!" I said.

"Well, I'll direct it, hahahahaha!" Director Gina said.

And then we stopped laughing and stared at each other. We looked at the calendar on the wall. We stared at each other again.

"The school year is almost over," I said.

"We have to act fast," she replied.

"Today is Wednesday."

"If you write it by Sunday, we can rehearse next week and open Friday."

So we did.

For the most part I felt nothing but scorn for an art form that required the pretense that it was natural for people to communicate with one another in rhymed song. Despite the many opportunities available to me in high school, the only musical I'd ever tried out for was *Grease*; after the auditions, during which I sinisterly hissed lines from the show like, "I don't know *why* I brought this *tire* iron, I coulda *ripped* those babies off with my *bare hands!*" the director cast me as Eugene, the gay geek, and then cut all the homophobic jokes, leaving me with virtually no part at all. The only musicals I'd done since then were Gilbert and Sullivan operettas, in which *every* character is a gay geek. I felt that the world already had more than enough Gilbert and Sullivan operettas, so we modeled our show on the only other musical I really liked, which was *Little Shop of Horrors,* a masterpiece that uses the ridiculousness inherent in the musical theater form to its advantage. We decided that our show, too, would revel in its own absurdity. We made Gina a tragic heroine and gave her a trio of backup singers, but instead of Chiffon, Crystal, and Ronnette (the names of the girls in the *Little Shop* trio), we called them Alecto, Megaera, and Tisiphone; they were the Furies of Greek legend, the immortals who pursue the wicked unto the ends of the earth to exact retribution for their crimes. Then we threw in Gina's abusive parents, her boyfriend, Harvard president Neil Rudenstine, his wife Angelica (who in our show wore a big pair of angel's wings cut out of poster board), an ensemble of Harvard admissions officers, and Joan of Arc's executioner (it was that kind of show).

For most of the musical numbers I just rewrote the lyrics to summer-camp songs or hits by the Shirelles:

GINA
Mama said there'll be days like this;
There'll be days like this, my mama said.

THE FURIES
Until you bludgeoned her to death!

But though I racked my brain and my CD collection, I couldn't find a song to steal for the turning point of the show; given the tight deadline, I finally gave up looking and wrote something myself. And it was kind of fabulous—"I know I'm just a little girl," six-year-old Gina sang, "but I've got dreams," and the music communicated something of the vulnerability of those dreams. When I played the song for her, Director Gina, who had studied at yeshiva, said, "Hebrew has two words for 'create,' *asah* and *bara.*"

"Okay," I said.

"*Asah* is to shape something out of something else that already exists. That's what I do as a director. The script is there already, I just bring it to life onstage." This made sense to me; *asah* was exactly what I did when, for example, my choir sang a piece composed by somebody else. "But *bara,*" Director Gina continued, "is to bring something into being out of nothing. I can't believe I'm saying something so cheesy, but I feel like that's kind of what you're doing here."

"*Asah* is making something from something else?"

"Right."

"And *bara* is making something from nothing?"

"Yes."

I furrowed my brow in thought. "Do you think you can figure out a way for the guy playing Alecto to have to have his shirt off for the entire show?"

We presented *G!* for two nights in a black box theater in the basement of my dorm with a cast made up of friends who owed me favors (and at first a guy I had a crush on—not the guy playing Alecto, a different guy—but he sent a clear signal by not showing up for the first rehearsal, so we fired him) and tape-recorded piano accompaniment. I played Tisiphone, in fishnets. Sixty or seventy people came to see the show, and they all loved it ("The best thing I've seen in thirty years," said a professor of mine afterward, though I'm not sure he would have been so effusive had he not been four or five sheets to the wind). The show ended with Gina Grant on a ladder, barred from climbing any farther. She sat down on the top step, sighed, and put a Columbia cap—the real Gina had not yet chosen a college—on her head.

I did not realize that in doing so she would change my life.

For most of my childhood I knew that when I grew up I wanted to be a cantor, the second-in-command who leads the sung prayers in synagogue. This filled my relatives with dismay, because rabbis, they explained, make much better money. It turned out not to be a problem, however, since, after the *Facts of Life* episode in which Mrs. Garrett's bakery burned down and was replaced by a gift shop, I realized that, although being a community's religious leader would be deeply fulfilling, the spiritual rewards it offered paled in comparison to those of running a boutique.

I changed my mind again after a meeting of the Charleston Young Musicians' Society. (If there had been a shred of doubt in anybody's mind that I was gay, my membership in the Charleston Young Musicians' Society should have removed it.) My friend Cathy's voice teacher Sam came to talk to us, and I have no recollection at all of what he said; I remember only that he was brilliant and terrifying. I began lessons with him and before very long it became clear to me that I was destined to be the greatest tenor in the world.

Strictly speaking, my desire was not so broad. I was not interested in the unsubtle opera written by Puccini and Wagner. Far more satisfying were the songs of Schubert and his ilk, composers who opened three-minute windows into the soul until syphilis turned them into gibbering madmen. But it was Baroque music that thrilled me to the marrow of my bones, music from the pens of Handel and Couperin and Bach, music of the early eighteenth century, music written in a time when everybody wore wigs but homeless stinking urchins, when *parfumiers* filled women's makeup with lead for its whitening properties, when singers shone more brightly in the firmament than kings. And the men who first sang this music were the most glamorous creatures ever to stride the earth. (Much of their glamour sprang from the castration they had undergone as children to preserve their soprano voices—audiences were known to cheer "long live the knife!"—but after very brief consideration I decided that, even though castrati could maintain erections and reach orgasm, there was still such a thing as going too far in the name of historically informed performance.) In later years I saw a sumptuous Belgian movie called *Farinelli,* based on the life of the most famous castrato of them all, and I have never forgotten a scene at the opera in which, approaching the climax of an aria, the title character suddenly stops singing and fixes his gaze—"icy" doesn't even begin to describe the malevolence in those eyes—on a woman in the audience whose attention is focused not on the stage but on the cup of tea in her right hand and the book in her left. She keeps reading for a moment and turns a page before realizing that the entire audience is staring at her, at which point she pales and sets her cup down, trembling so violently she almost overturns it. Farinelli smiles coldly and starts the aria again. After the opera is over she sends him her diamond necklace and then he publicly and viciously rejects her sexual advances.

Who wouldn't wish to command such power?

Furthermore, the lyrical and musical language of Baroque music is extravagant, unequivocal, full of lines like *The serpent, once insulted, rests not until his venom spreads through his enemy's blood* and *Come, my son, and console me; but if life is forbidden you, at least die on my breast,* lines that allow the singer to cry out with the fullness of every honest emotion and at the same time to refine each of those emotions to its noblest state. Anger, love, despair, joy, hatred: the alchemy in this music transmutes them into gold that fills the voice.

But as I improved—Sam was a very good teacher—I began to discover an even deeper desire underneath the hunger for glory and purity of feeling. One week the supplemental reading in my high school English class (I was the kind of teenager who did the supplemental reading in my high school English class) was Edgar Allan Poe's "The Poetic Principle," and in it I found the following lines:

> It is in Music perhaps that the soul most nearly attains . . . the creation of supernal Beauty. We are often made to feel, with a shivering delight, that from an earthly harp are stricken notes which *cannot* have been unfamiliar to the angels.

Manic-depressive, laudanum-addled, Poe had captured the essence of what I longed for. And that's the amazing thing about singing: when you do it right, *you are that earthly harp.* If you can let the notes come not from you but through you, if you can empty yourself of pride and cunning and rodomontade, then you leave room for music to fill you, to melt everything in you that is not holy, to lift you up and fling you to the farthest reaches of human possibility.

Not that I did it right all or even much of the time. But occasionally I came close. A few years after my first professional gig I was giving a concert in a Boston chapel with an acoustic that softened every sound in it. "Gentle airs, melodious strains," I sang, my voice caressing every molecule of air in the room as even the dust motes shimmered in the setting July sun, "call for raptures out of woe," and the melisma on the word "woe" floated higher and higher and then higher still, and I felt I could sustain it forever, and my body disappeared and I understood what it is to be eternal.

Until my junior year of college, that is, when I lost all physical sensation in the back of my throat.

I could still produce a pretty tone; I just couldn't perform the subtle manipulations of the vocal apparatus necessary for glorious singing, because I couldn't feel the vocal apparatus.

And I spent the next two anguished years in the offices of doctors none of whom could figure out what the fuck was going on, not even the really really hot one who waited just a moment too long to release my hand when he introduced himself and whose subsequent failure to heal me was therefore an even greater betrayal than the failures of all the others, and I woke up every morning crying and I wrote overwrought letters to my friends during the summer (this was before e-mail) about how my own body was cutting me off from my destiny. Luckily I had very forbearing friends but still.

And then finally somebody diagnosed me with severe gastric reflux and told me the acid shooting up from my stomach into my throat had done so much damage my voice would never come back.

At which point nothing was easier than emptying myself of pride and cunning and rodomontade, but what filled me was not music but despair. Also chocolate, so that in the end I wasn't just miserable; I was miserable and fat.

And I sleepwalked through my life, not really paying attention, because why bother, and I graduated from college and applied for teaching jobs and didn't get any. And I figured maybe I could go to grad school somewhere or become a lawyer even though my dad the civil rights lawyer who'd won every case he'd ever argued before the Supreme Court said he didn't want me to be a lawyer because he thought I could do better, but I *couldn't* do better, I'd tried and I *couldn't*. And when they'd assigned *Steppenwolf* in high school I'd memorized the part about living with such strength and indescribable beauty that the spray of your moment's happiness could be flung so high and dazzlingly over the wide sea of suffering that the light of it, spreading its radiance, might touch others too with its enchantment, but that wasn't an option anymore so instead I'd just have to tread water in the sea of suffering until I drowned and it was just too fucking bad.

And then one day in the midst of this agony I was having dinner with a slightly kooky older friend with long fingernails who had once dated my father and all at once she said, "I just had a psychic vision! I saw you at age twenty-seven and you were surrounded by light and you were incredibly happy."

And I said, "Was I a singer?"

And she said, "No. I don't know what you were doing, but whatever it was, you felt totally fulfilled."

And I understood all at once, as I headed back to the salad bar despite the fact that they had run out of Baco Bits, that *I could do something else with my life and still be happy.* And I felt the tar pit that had been sucking me relentlessly into its depths begin to liquefy and I realized I had been given back my liberty and my life and I didn't know yet what I was going to do with them, maybe I'd establish world peace or find a cure for AIDS or hatred or maybe I'd grow wings and fly, because I could do any of those things, and then I asked my friend an even more important question, which was, "Do I have a boyfriend, and is he blond?"

To my dismay, she said she hadn't seen whether I had a boyfriend or not, because I had been so complete in her vision as I was. I found this a deeply unsatisfactory answer but it was clearly the best I was going to get.

I spent the next few days trying to figure out what I wanted to do now that I didn't have to do what my stomach wouldn't let me do. I blathered to my father about my options; I blathered to friends; I blathered to strangers at the pizza parlor. I was paralyzed with indecision. How could I possibly choose a path? Any door I approached would open at my knock; after all, I was smart and funny and could type eighty-five words a minute.

And then I remembered how much fun I'd had writing *G!* and working on it with Director Gina. Perhaps, I thought, I should become a writer of musical theater. I called a friend in NYU's Graduate Musical Theater Writing Program, and he couldn't endorse it highly enough. So I decided to apply and, at the same time, to try writing a full-length musical. A thirty-minute jeu d'esprit is one thing; sustaining both the jeu and the esprit over the course of an evening, however, might be entirely beyond my reach. For one thing, what would I write about? How could I possibly top teenage matricidal Harvard applicants?

The answer was: with *Princess Di: A Fairy Tale* (written before Diana's tragic death), in which the Furies came back for a repeat engagement, joined this time by Carmen Miranda, Ed McMahon, Maleficent the witch from *Sleeping Beauty,* Lady Macbeth, McDonald's Grimace, and a chorus of reporters named Nigel. Director Gina directed brilliantly, one of my friends dressed in drag to play Camilla Parker-Bowles, and for the show's finale I turned a Bach chorale into a rousing gospel number. The Graduate Musical Theater Writing Program accepted me and I moved to New York.

Musical theater, more than any other art form, forces its practitioners to collaborate. Lerner and Loewe, Rodgers and Hammerstein, Bock and Harnick—the people who write successfully almost never write alone. Even when one person writes music and lyrics, somebody else usually writes the script (Sondheim and Weidman, Finn and Lapine, Herman and Stewart). The Musical Theater Writing Program trained its students for this reality by insisting that, for the two years we were under its tutelage, each of us choose to focus on either music or words, as we would do most of our work in collaboration with other students.

I found this profoundly annoying; I didn't need to collaborate with anybody, because I already knew everything. All the same, I did not wish to gain a reputation as a troublemaker, so I enrolled as a composer.

And no matter which lyricist I was working with, I brought in the same goddamn song every week. I used the same six chords (four, really, since two were variations) over and over again whether the song was about a Southern beauty pageant contestant or a town overrun by zombies or a war between a gang of chickens and a gang of frogs, and before long everyone had begun to dread my workshop presentations, me most of all. The music I wrote shone extravagantly and unambiguously, just like the Baroque music I had sung with such passion, yet more and more it illuminated nothing but the paucity of my imagination. I was writing the musical equivalent of lead and I was helpless to transmute it into anything that contained even a hint of gold.

Finally, one evening in my second semester, after sitting in a practice room writing for an hour and a half and coming up with the same song yet again, this time for a character whose husband was about to be shipped off to war, I found one of my professors. "I can't stand this song anymore," I said, dragging him to the piano. "Can you help me write something different?"

"Thank *God,*" he said. "Okay. Play a few chords."

I did, and three of my six standards came out. "See? It's just gross."

"Hold your horses. Now take your hands off the keyboard and wiggle your fingers around." I did. "Now, *without looking at the keyboard,* and *without shaping a chord ahead of time with your fingers,* put your hands down again." I did, and the piano emitted a bizarre, hideous sound. I made a face. "Do you like that?"

"No."

"Okay. Try it again." I put my hands down, produced a different bizarre, hideous sound, and made another face. "One more time." And this time the sound that rang from the hammered strings was bizarre . . . but not hideous.

In fact, it was kind of interesting. It was full of instability, ambivalence, doubt.

I looked down at my hands to see what notes they had struck to create the sound still echoing faintly in the air. The chord made complete theoretical sense; it just wasn't anything I would ever have written on purpose. I scribbled the notes down and tried again. When I had found three or four chords I liked, I started playing with accompaniment patterns: Should the fingers of the right hand stay still while those of the left hand moved? Should both move at the same time but in opposite directions? Then I looked at the words my collaborator for the week had given me and considered possibilities for the vocal melody over the accompaniment. *Once more, you must go,* the lyric began, *and I pull you tight.* The musical line that came out was slow and tentative, almost in denial. My professor and I kept going, and by the end of the evening I had written a song that sounded like nothing I'd ever composed before. This was *bara,* what Director Gina had defined as bringing something into being out of nothingness. Certainly my previous songs had been the products of *bara* as well, but this felt fundamentally different—this felt vast, immeasurable. It wasn't a completely comfortable experience, but I felt nonetheless a bubbling excitement utterly different from the joy of *asah* that had filled me when I sang. When I brought the new song in to workshop the next day my classmates applauded wildly, not because it was such a great song but because for once I hadn't subjected them to the six chords they had come to know and loathe.

More important than the actual sound the pianist and the singer produced, however, was my growing understanding that I had been wrong about musical theater. A form in which characters feel emotions so powerfully the spoken word is insufficient to express them is not stupid; it's revelatory. Yip Harburg, the lyricist for *The Wizard of Oz,* said, "Words make you think a thought. Music makes you feel a feeling. A song makes you feel a thought." I don't think there's anything else on earth that can do that.

And along with my changing perspective on the form itself, I also began to learn that, in a piece of theater, a song doesn't have the luxury of just sounding pretty, of just expressing love or rage or despair; it also has a job to do, in helping a character make or fail to make an emotional journey. Whether or not you want to hear it on the radio isn't quite as important. In the year after my musical prison break, I set lyrics like this one by my friend Diana to music as unresolved as I could manage:*

> *Last night we spent an hour on the phone.*
> *We talked about our friends, and moaned about our jobs,*
> *And laughed about the villain on that stupid TV show.*
> *I hoped your voice would fill the empty spaces in my heart,*
> *But all I heard was what you weren't saying,*
> *And I don't know if those words will ever start.*

For a song in which Lizzie Borden went mad, I wrote music in two different keys at the same time (imagine the dreadful sound of the first lines of "Happy Birthday" as sung by any large group before everybody starts singing the same notes, but lasting throughout the song and in fact getting more and more dreadful as the character's sanity slips further and further away).

The project that takes much of my focus these days is a musical drama I'm writing with a brilliant lyricist named Len Schiff and a brilliant scriptwriter named Peter Ullian about Terezin, the concentration camp the Nazis filled with artists

*http://www.joelderfner.com/music/files/I_Don't_Know.mp3

and musicians and intellectuals and then used as a propaganda tool to show the rest of the world how well Hitler was treating the Jews.

Whenever I tell people I'm writing a musical about a concentration camp, their brows wrinkle in disbelief. "What, with singing Nazis?" they say. "Why on earth would you want to write a musical about the Holocaust?"

To which my answer is that we're not writing a musical about the Holocaust. *Terezin* is about what happens when art is co-opted by tyranny, about how people can assert their freedom when they are not free, about what truths might be worth dying for. We're telling a story of the triumph of creation over despair. And where else should we tell this story but in a concentration camp, because where else but in the face of absolute cruelty do courage, generosity, and kindness put the forces of destruction more thoroughly to rout?

We do have singing Nazis in our musical, though they don't sing much. But the song the younger one sings is among my favorites in the show, because often the most terrifying villain is the one who doesn't know he's a villain:*

> *And to the ones who cry compassion,*
> *Preaching, "Hate is not the answer,"*
> *I say humans must hate Jews*
> *The way the surgeon hates the cancer:*
> *He reserves his share of pity*
> *For preserving human life—*
> *Attentive to his cause,*
> *Unswerving with his knife.*

*http://www.joelderfner.com/music/files/Good.mp3

When I saw this lyric, full of hate and anger, I understood that the worst musical response would be to set it to hateful, angry chords. Because it's not illuminating at all to write music that communicates what *I* feel about the character; I have to communicate what the character feels about himself. So the music is some of the sweetest, most lyrical that I've ever written—and the song is *really* creepy, because the audience sees not a cardboard cutout but a man whose noblest impulses have so decayed that he can't even recognize what he's become.

And ultimately that nobility and that decay are the reasons I write musicals. What's playing on Broadway now? *Mamma Mia,* a totally fun, campy show written around the songs of ABBA. *Hairspray,* a totally fun, campy adaptation of the John Waters movie, short on subversion but long on delight. And I really enjoyed these shows when I saw them, and God knows we need all the fun we can get. But if musical theater stops there, if its writers remain silent about the corruption and wickedness and greed around us, then we are complicit in our own destruction and in the destruction of everything we hold dear. "If I write about a hill that is rotting," declared Wyndham Lewis in the introduction to his collection of stories *The Rotting Hill,* "it is because I despise rot." If composers and lyricists and playwrights allow rot to pass unremarked, we are wasting our opportunities and squandering our talent. Hitler is dead and the Nazis are no more, but as far as I can see, our leaders still manipulate us and poison us and sacrifice us on the altar of their power, and if people who see *Terezin* aren't led to consider the parallels, then Len and Peter and I have done our job badly.

Near the end of the show, the heroine, Lorelei, comes to believe that the Nazis have destroyed all the sketches she made of her friends and family. But in the last scene, after the war is over, she finds the drawings secreted away throughout the camp, hidden by other inmates between bricks, behind shingles, under floorboards. During a recent rehearsal for a production outside of Seattle, as I watched Lorelei learn that through her creation something of her loved ones still lived,

what I was thinking about was *Moon Landscape*. In 2002, Israeli astronaut Ilan Ramon asked the Jerusalem Holocaust memorial for an artifact to take into space; they gave him a drawing by Petr Ginz, who at fourteen had been an inmate of Terezin. Ramon had *Moon Landscape* with him on the space shuttle *Columbia* when it blew up over Texas on February 1, 2003, what would have been Ginz's seventy-fifth birthday.

A few days after the *Columbia* disaster I read that the only living things to survive the rain of aluminum and flesh and mystery into which the shuttle had exploded were some worms. They were *C. elegans,* apparently the first multicellular organism whose genome scientists mapped completely, which was why they had been taken into space in a container that later fell to earth intact—researchers wanted to find out how reproduction over multiple generations in space affected the species.

It turns out, I learned, that *C. elegans* is hermaphroditic; it reproduces itself. Maybe, I thought, this means it's whole in a way no *Homo sapiens,* gay or straight, can ever be, because it can just keep going and going past the end of time with no help from anybody or anything, while if we can't love one another and annoy one another and have sweaty awkward sex with one another we die for good.

Petr Ginz was murdered in Auschwitz two years after he drew *Moon Landscape,* so he never got any closer to the moon he drew than the *Columbia* astronauts did. Still, I hope that on that February day in 2003 his picture was ripped into seven billion pieces, one for every person on this planet, and flung just like in *Steppenwolf* so high and dazzlingly over the wide sea of suffering that the light of his *bara,* spreading its radiance, might touch us all with its enchantment. I believe that the planet visible in this drawing has never known mounds of gold fillings from Jewish teeth, or the castration of singing children, or Matthew Shepard tied to a fence, or the Janjaweed rape of black women in the Sudan, or husbands and lovers and children leaping from the windows of the World Trade Center. And so if Petr Ginz, who saw around him in Terezin an endlessly renewed mass of people sent daily to the slaughter, still imagined a planet without cruelty—and I hope fervently that he did—then he committed the boldest act of *bara* since God breathed life into Adam in Genesis 2:7.

We will end up food for *C. elegans* no matter what. But our souls are immortal, and I think reaching for that immortality when it can never be achieved is the greatest gesture of creation in the world. When Petr Ginz and all the other artists in Terezin, who had nothing—no food, no supplies, no dignity—used that nothing to create hope, they made themselves immortal, while the world exploded, by reaching for one another and for us.

A few months ago I was in Chicago, visiting old friends (theirs was the first lesbian wedding I ever attended), and one day one of them said, "Hey, listen. A singer friend of mine had a really bad case of gastric reflux, and she went to a specialist who did some new kind of treatment that completely cured her. Do you want me to get you his contact information?"

I said, "No, thanks. I'm happier doing what I'm doing now. I don't want to go back there."

I was lying.

The loss of *asah* haunts me. If there is nothing like the joy of writing a piece of music and hearing it come out of an actor's throat for the first time, there is also no getting around the fact that it's somebody else's throat the music is coming out of, somebody else who is Poe's earthly harp. I compose with my mind, and feel pride and satisfaction; I sang with my body, and felt ecstasy. Music doesn't exist without a performer—notes on a page are not music, any more than a recipe is dinner—and so when you are composing you are powerless to give your creation a soul. The act of creating is separated from the act of bringing to life. But when you're singing, you're not only molding something from what already exists; *you are what is being molded.* You are creator and created at the same time, thrumming with the breath of life, reaching out to everybody on earth and feeling everybody on earth reach back. For *bara* you need faith that one day someone will read or look at or hear what you have made and be changed. But when you engage in *asah,* that day is *today.* You don't need faith, because your audience changes in front of your eyes, and, in changing, changes you too.

The choir in Terezin petitioned the commander of the camp to delay a transport to Auschwitz so that the singers destined for the gas chambers could perform the Verdi *Requiem* before they died. They knew what awaited them, and they knew the world didn't care, so they couldn't have been motivated by pragmatism. Of course they can't tell us what drove them but I choose to believe that, after their request was approved, as they stood and sang "Lord, grant them eternal rest," understanding that the words were as far from rhetorical as they would ever be, they were transmuted by the spray of their moment's happiness into gold so pure no crematorium could ever destroy it.

When my lesbians went to the movies a few hours after

our conversation about their singer friend, I didn't join them, even though I had heard Hugh Jackman spent a lot of time onscreen with his shirt off. Instead, I sat at their piano and worked on a trio I was writing for *Terezin*. I'd already written the basic shape of the song, so I started playing with the different voices, bringing this one in here, taking that one a sixth higher there, joining all three in unison for a line before splitting them into dissonance with a resolution so unexpected it made me laugh with glee when I discovered it. Eventually I reached a natural stopping point in my work, but I didn't get up from the piano.

It was certainly possible, I thought, that I could go to my friend's friend's specialist and he might wave his magic tongue depressor and give me back what I had lost. But it was also possible that he might wave the tongue depressor and *nothing would happen,* at which point I would be unable to bear breathing any longer.

Because the glee I feel when I surprise myself composing is real, but I feel it only because I have lulled to sleep the memory of what infinity feels like; and I am afraid of what might happen if I woke that memory up. I love my life because a part of me has learned how to give up hope, and that, I suspect, is a dangerous lesson to unlearn.

As I sat at my friends' piano my fingers eventually assumed a position they had not held for years, and then I opened my mouth: "Gentle airs, melodious strains," I sang, picturing the dust motes shimmering in a Boston chapel. But when I got to the next part, when I was supposed to sing "call for raptures out of woe," neither my hands nor my throat could remember what to do.

On Go-Go Dancing

"*H*ow's the book going?" my friend Jim asked over Indian food.

"Bleah," I said in between forkfuls of beef samosa. "Mostly it's fine, but I'm worried. I feel like there's some aspect of gay life I haven't tapped into. And if the book isn't perfect then everyone who reads it will hate me. Maybe I'm not gay enough."

Jim couldn't respond right away, as he had gotten something caught in his throat that seemed to require a great deal of coughing to dislodge, but when he had regained his composure he told me he had faith I'd come up with something. Then he started talking about the sketchy party he had been to on New Year's Eve. "It was in a restaurant," he said, "and there were a bunch of naked go-go boys dancing with hard-ons, and people were sucking each other off in dark corners. Then there was a competition to find America's Next Top Bottom." During the fit of uncontrollable laughter into which this sent me, Jim joked that I should become a go-go boy and write about that, but I didn't pay attention, because all I could think about was racing home and Googling "America's Next Top Bottom." When I finally did so I found, among other things, a blog kept by a go-go boy who had attended the party, though he had not competed to be America's Next Top Bottom. His account of the event was delicious, and in general his experiences as a go-go boy sounded, if not entirely wholesome, at least exciting. ("Though Jack was talking with someone and getting blown by someone else, he absentmindedly stroked my cock until it was rock-hard. I ran the back of my hand over his backside, which was incredibly smooth.")

And then Jim's words came back to me and I started thinking: What if he was right? What if I should become a go-go boy? What if an exploration of gay nightlife was truly what my book needed to be whole? What if it was what *I* needed to be whole?

But I was being ridiculous. Go-go dancers were muscled, sexy, carefree, and young. I was no longer overweight but I couldn't imagine that the musculature required for dancing in underwear was anywhere close to within my reach. Furthermore, I felt as sexy as Kermit the Frog, I was as carefree as Job, and at thirty-three I was already cheating death in gay years.

And yet.

The more of Go-Go Boy's blog I read, the more compelling I found the idea, especially after I realized that he was just a working stiff who'd started dancing for fun a few months before the party Jim had attended. *What if I could actually do this?* I wondered.

It was difficult to picture myself writhing on a bar. For my first thirty years I had held the life of the body beneath contempt. In kindergarten I had been so absorbed in the puzzle map of Africa I was taking back to the map drawer that I didn't realize Samara Zinn had tripped me until I was flat on my face, former French and English protectorates mingling indiscriminately about me on the floor. My first-grade T-ball team put me deep in the outfield because I was too busy picking flowers to pay any attention to the ball. A photo of me at twenty-eight shows a sphere standing in a theater lobby, my porcine fingers barely able to close around the playbill. I had stayed away from the world of gay clubs because my only strengths were my intellectual ones, which were imperceptible in the dark no matter how many cosmopolitans men around me had consumed. Though I was now aware for the first time that I possessed physical mass, it was not an aspect of myself with which I felt at all comfortable. And I was considering a career as a sex object?

I sought out a former professor of mine, not unacquainted with the seedier side of gay life, and asked him what he thought. "Lift up your shirt," he said, and I did. "Yeah, you could do it."

"But aren't go-go boys all like nineteen years old?" I asked.

"No," he said.

"But aren't they all big muscle jocks?"

"A lot of them are," he said, "but some of them are small and lean like you." He named half a dozen bars at which somebody with my body type might find a warm welcome and sent me on my way.

The one remaining problem was that I did not know how to become a go-go boy. If there was a graduate school I was unaware of it. The Learning Annex did not offer classes. But then I figured, *It's a job, right? I know how to apply for jobs.* So I e-mailed Go-Go Boy, praising his blog, and asked him for the contact information of the people who hired dancers at the clubs where he worked.

His puzzled response read, "Um, usually I just get gigs by showing up and asking the party promoters if they'll let me audition for them then and there. I guess you could get in touch with some of them and tell them you want to try out. Here are numbers and e-mails for a few of the guys who throw parties on different nights at different clubs."

The first part of this explanation was of course inconceivable; I could no more show up at a club and ask to audition than I could translate the complete works of Betty Friedan into Linear A. I had crossed the threshold of a gay bar fewer than a dozen times. The night my friend Stephen wanted to take me to my first New York club I agreed to go only if he didn't make me check my copy of *The Count of Monte Cristo* with my jacket. The most adventurous of my bar visits came a few days after Tom and I broke up, when I took a cab to Hell's Kitchen, walked into a bar alone for the first time, ordered a Diet Coke, slurped it up through the tiny bar straw without making eye contact with anybody, and fled.

However, I write cover letters (and make query phone calls) like nobody's business. I hit a snag when no matter how hard I tried I could not find the specifications for a properly formatted go-go-boy résumé. Then I realized that I had no relevant experience to list on such a résumé anyway so the only thing I could do was make first contact and improvise from there. Between e-mail and the telephone I shot off half a dozen requests for auditions.

And got no reply.

Then one guy, named either Benjamin or Antoine—it wasn't clear which—called me back and said yes, he was looking for go-go dancers, I should send him some photos. I had my boyfriend Mike take some pictures of me in the shower and e-mailed them immediately to Benjamantoine.

And got no reply.

This was the worst thing that had ever happened to me. People I had never met heard my voice or saw my picture or read my impeccable typing and hated me. The fact that my book was obviously doomed to fail was the least of my worries; my ego was at stake. Despite a life spent avoiding bars, I had begun to tie my self-image to the idea of being their cynosure. I spent week after week in therapy talking about my inability to get a job as a go-go boy. "All I want is to become a piece of meat," I complained to my therapist. "Why is that so difficult?" He suggested that party promoters were unlikely to be as responsible about communication as most people I was used to dealing with. I suggested that he was missing the point; he suggested that we talk about my mother.

I thought about Go-Go Boy obsessively. Eventually, after continuing our electronic conversation for a while, we met for dinner, and I didn't see what was so great about him. He was an inch or two taller than me, with short brown hair and a cute nose. Nothing especially out of the ordinary. Yet according to his blog he was dancing all the time and making heaps of money. I pictured him spending every night in the throes of sybaritic ecstasy and then going home confident in the knowledge that he had the power to make a bar full of men want him. Ordinarily I would have been able to say, well, he may be a better go-go boy than me, but I went to Harvard. I couldn't do that in this case, though, because *he did too.* He was pleasant and kind and went out of his way to be helpful to me, and I prayed for the earth to open up and swallow him whole.

And then finally—*yes!*—somebody e-mailed me back. His name was Daniel, and he was the very man who had thrown the New Year's Eve party with which my friend Jim had set this all in motion. "Come by Splash some Wednesday and audition for me," he wrote, so a few nights later I went to bed early, woke up to my alarm at midnight, and took the subway down to New York's best-known gay club. I showed the doorman my driver's license and, keeping my fingers crossed, pulled the door open.

I stepped into a room where sex suffused the very air. Everywhere I looked, I saw men chatting at the bar, men adjusting their coiffures in the ubiquitous mirrors, men dancing with an abandon reached either by sheer will or by very good drugs, thrusting their hips in time to the wild *thump-thump-thump* of the music. The shirtless bartenders, smiling flirtatiously, handed drinks to patrons who then turned back to one another and recommenced devouring one another's lips with the fierceness of leopards. And on a platform in the middle were two go-go boys, haughty, aloof, unapproachable. One was tall and blond, muscles bulging in places muscles shouldn't be allowed to exist; the other was shorter, black, compact and tight. They danced together as if they were the only two people in the world. I hungered to fulfill my newly discovered destiny, to leave behind the troubles of the common folk and join the aristocracy of the gay demimonde, in whose company I would be transformed into an animal of such raging heat that men would have to avert their eyes in my presence or be burned to ash. Then out of the corner of my eye I saw a composer who'd won three awards I'd applied for, and I had to hide behind a column so he wouldn't see me.

In order to audition for Daniel I first had to find him, but I had no idea what he looked like. I approached the shorter go-go boy on the platform and, since it seemed rude to ask for information without offering anything in return, stuck a dollar in his underwear. "DO YOU KNOW WHERE DANIEL IS?" I screamed in his ear over the deafening music.

"SDFDZXUYVILJSJIUHVLE!" he screamed back.

"HUNH?" I screamed, and he screamed again; if my life had depended on it I could not have identified a single morpheme. I thanked him and trudged off to repeat this conversation with increasingly intimidating go-go boys and patrons alike for forty-five minutes, both on the ground floor and on the lower level, until at last somebody took pity on me, led me through the crowd, and introduced me to Daniel. The man I had been searching for was tall, with a long face and dark brown hair; he said it was nice to meet me and told me to get up on the bar near the entrance and start dancing, so I did.

I was instantly filled with terror that I would get it wrong and that people would laugh at me. What the fuck did I know? I should get down immediately and go home and eat ice cream while Googlestalking old boyfriends. Scratch that; eat ice cream and M&M's while Googlestalking old boyfriends.

Clear your mind, I told myself firmly. *Focus on details to remember when you write about this.* I did so, and I was instantly filled with terror that I would focus on the wrong details and that when I sat down at the computer all I would remember would be the bar's gaudy decorative scheme, so I went back to being filled with terror that I would get it wrong and thinking about ice cream and M&M's and Googlestalking old boyfriends.

But eventually I began to relax. The great thing about go-go dancing, it turns out, is that you don't actually have to dance. In fact, you barely have to move at all. My boyfriend, Mike, who is a great dancer, had attempted to teach me some impressive moves before my audition, but he went too fast and made me cry, so I stuck with the basics: stepping languidly from foot to foot, gyrating at the hip, and sometimes running one hand or the other over my pectoral muscles. Every couple of minutes I moved a foot and a half to my left and stepped and gyrated and ran there. The terror subsided—how could it not, when men were looking up and smiling at my nearly naked body?—but neither did I feel transported to the higher state of being I had expected to reach. Possibly this had something to do with the fact that I kept having to apologize to people for kicking their drinks over.

After I'd traversed six feet of the narrow bar, a well-dressed guy grinned at me, pulled out his wallet, removed a dollar bill from it, folded it in half as I bent my knees to get within arm's length, and tentatively put it behind the band of the skimpy underwear I had bought expressly for this audition. I stood up, gave him a smile that I hoped hit the halfway mark between sweet and salacious, and moved on. His physical properties were different from those that usually attract me to a man. But still something in me thrilled at having stepped into a land where the laws governing the sunlit world held no sway. If I had been at a movie theater and somebody had come up to me and shoved his hand into my underpants, I would have been disconcerted (though not necessarily upset, depending on how cute he was). But in this bar, whose denizens breathed not oxygen but alcohol and sweat and desire, such a gesture was no less decorous than a handshake.

An hour later, when the official go-go boys started to leave, I had five dollar bills in my underwear. I wanted desperately to ask Daniel whether this was a good sum of money to have earned or a bad sum of money to have earned, but I suspected the latter and I feared he would scorn me, so I just nodded to him on my way down to the clothes check. As I bent to put my pants back on, I realized that when I'd banged my knee against the column on the bar I'd actually gashed it open, and blood was oozing down my leg (this had happened only minutes earlier so unfortunately it did not explain the bad tips). When I got home I showed Mike the wound, which he immediately started calling my go-go boo-boo.

I couldn't sleep, so afire with excitement was I. During a

rapid flurry of suggestive e-mails with Daniel it became clear that my audition had gone well and that I was on my way to go-go-boy superstardom. Then at one point he asked, "How would you feel about dancing naked?" and I e-mailed back that I would have to ask my boyfriend and Daniel didn't write back, which worried me. I asked Mike the next day and he said he was fine with my dancing naked, so I e-mailed Daniel again and told him so, adding, for good measure, "I haven't been this excited since Madonna's performance of 'Vogue' at the MTV Awards in 1990!!!!!!" Daniel maintained e-silence. Finally, after weeks of torment, I decided that he was not interested in hiring me unless I was available for fooling around. This made a welcome change for my therapist, since now instead of talking about how I was failing to become a go-go boy I could talk about how it was my own goddamn fault I was failing to become a go-go boy and how by admitting that I had a boyfriend I had ruined my life. I hated Go-Go Boy more viciously than ever, even as I searched and searched his blog for the key to his sortilege. Finally, in a moment of inspiration, I e-mailed Daniel again and told him that Mike and I had broken up, which was a lie, and within a day he had written back and asked whether I could work a party that weekend.

The party, to be held in the outdoors on a pier by the Hudson River, celebrated the opening of a gay media conference. I would not actually be dancing; instead, I would just wander around in my underwear. It rained the whole day of the party and after it stopped raining the air was still bitter cold, so Daniel wrote and told me I didn't have to come if I didn't want to, especially as the gig didn't pay. I ignored this, since I would have shown up if the party had been in Pompeii and Vesuvius had been showing signs of disquietude.

When I got to the pier and stripped down to my thong,

however, I panicked. This was my first official engagement as a go-go boy and I had no idea what to do. I called Mike, frantic.

"You're going to be great," he said.

"But what if they hate me?"

"You're so sexy. They're going to love you."

"You have to say that, you're my boyfriend. What if I have to *talk* to people?"

"Just act like a very sweet, very nice, not very intelligent twink. Pretend like you're pretending to know what they're talking about. You know"—here his voice turned vacuous—" 'Oh, really? I think my cousin did that once. Where did you get that jacket?' "

This sounded exactly right, so I went back to the party and within twenty minutes had ensnared myself in conversations about the differences between Judaism and Shinto, the virtues and flaws of two different productions of Handel's *Acis and Galatea,* and the constitutionality of jury nullification.

Then one guy started talking to me about the party he'd been to recently on the tugboat tied next to us on the pier. "It's a really cool boat," he said. "Do you want to go see it?"

"Sure," I said, and for five seconds I actually thought he wanted to show me the tugboat. Then we stepped aboard and he pulled me to him and started biting my neck.

I had never found the romance-novel phrase "he pulled her to him" credible when it described the action the arrogant yet compelling nobleman performed upon the plucky serving-maid heroine, but now, in a flash, I understood. The power of attraction calls to something deeper than human volition, and more shadowed. Though I found the fellow in front of me moderately sexy, I had no interest in being unfaithful to my boyfriend. Yet this man's desire was a tractor beam, drawing me not just toward him but also away from an existence in which I had ever been the object of anyone's derision, away from the kindergarten room in which I had crouched on the floor picking up pieces of the puzzle map, cheeks burning, trying to remember whether Zaire went above or below Angola and hating Samara Zinn's guts.

If I had the opportunity on this tugboat to leave her behind, even for a moment, how could I not seize it?

So my new friend bit my neck and ran his hands over my back and squeezed my ass and tried to kiss my lips, though I wouldn't let him, and I watched the misshapen self he couldn't see grow fainter and fainter, until it was almost more fantasy than reality, instead of the other way around. But when he became more daring, I forced myself to say, "We need to stop; I have a boyfriend."

"I'll behave myself," he said, "I'll really behave myself," which I took to be about as honest as "He won't mind if you eat the apple" or "We found the weapons of mass destruction." Then he reached down between us and I said, "No, we really have to stop, 'cause you're so hot I'm not going to be able to control myself otherwise." This is my standard lie when I want to deflect a man's advances without offending him, except that it's never completely a lie, even if he isn't somebody I want to spend the rest of my life with, because the specter of Samara is always with me and any chance to forget her seems a chance worth taking.

So I pulled away from him, regretfully but firmly, and led him back to the party, which lasted another couple hours and during the busiest part of which I was given the job of leading performers to the radio-show booth after their sets were done.

Then I went home, fell asleep, and woke up the next day racked with guilt that I had let a man touch me who wasn't my boyfriend.

During the aerobics class I taught that morning, I was so worried about how Mike would react when I told him what had happened that I paid no attention to what I was doing and almost caused one of my students to fracture her tibia. At lunch afterward, however, what Mike said was, "I don't have a problem with it. I know how that world works, and I understand the difference between what you give them and what you give me. If you started engaging these guys sexually, I'd feel uncomfortable, but that's not what this was about. I feel secure in our relationship, and I trust you."

(When I relayed this conversation to my friend Jim later on the phone he was silent for a moment and then he screamed into the receiver, "DON'T YOU DARE FUCK THIS RELATIONSHIP UP!")

The next day, Daniel asked whether I could be the regular go-go boy for his Saturday-night radio show; apparently I had performed my task of walking people twenty feet in a straight line with such aplomb as to make clear that here was someone who could be depended upon. "I can pay you a hundred dollars a show," he said. I did not understand why a radio show needed a go-go boy—were people supposed to *hear* me running my hands over my pectoral muscles?—but it was clearly a leg up and I needed the money and besides who wouldn't want to be paid for sitting around in his underwear? My chief responsibility turned out to be mixing drinks for the guests, a duty I discharged admirably, since I believe the correct way to make a cocktail (learned from my mother) is to fill the glass to overflowing with spirits and then wave the mixer somewhere vaguely near the rim.

At my first show I had a moment of panic when I mentioned the book I had written, *Gay Haiku,* and Daniel's cohost, not aware that I was claiming to be single, revealed that his next-door neighbor had told him her brother was dating the author of that book. "Are you still going out with him?" Matthew asked, threatening unwittingly to expose my deception.

"Um," I mumbled, "it's complicated," and refused to say any more. The next morning I called Mike's sister and forbade her to mention me to anybody until further notice.

But over the next few Saturdays I realized I'd been completely wrong about Daniel and that he couldn't have cared less whether I was single or not. The better I got to know him, in fact, the more generous and genuine I realized he was. ("You think too much," he said genially as he bought me dinner one night. "It's not attractive.") Furthermore, working for him brought me into contact with people I could never have predicted I would meet and admire. The aptitude test I had taken in tenth grade did not suggest that I would one day be all but naked in a radio booth laughing as I handed piña coladas to drag queens and bons vivants and lesbian punk-rock bands. "You have weird jobs," Mike told me one evening, but I heard pride in his voice.

Yet I still felt like a failure. I was wilting in the shadow of Go-Go Boy. I had danced in my underwear and been tipped, and I had been paid to take most of my clothes off, but the two had yet to be combined in the same endeavor, and I understood that it was because I wasn't good enough and I never would be.

But then Daniel finally called and asked whether I could dance at Splash the following Wednesday, and relief washed over me like a very small, benign tsunami. There was no W-2 to fill out, no photo ID to process, but I would nevertheless be a real live go-go dancer.

On the appointed night I set out for Chelsea at eleven; I arrived late, but within thirty seconds of my getting up on the bar, somebody had reached into my underwear, given what he found there a quick squeeze, and pulled his hand out, leaving a twenty behind. Clearly this was not going to be a five-dollar night.

I went on in this manner until the wee hours of the morning. I moved lazily from one end of the bar to the other, smiling coyly at men until they pulled out their wallets. Every so often my underwear would fill up and I'd have to stuff most of the money in my socks. Then my socks would fill up and I'd have to go put most of the money in my locker. Occasionally men would ask my name and tell me theirs and we would spend a few moments talking, but mostly they chose to tip in appreciative silence.

And for three and a half hours, I wasn't worried.

About anything.

Because no one was weighing me in the balance, eager to find me wanting. No one was trying to determine whether or not I was sexy, because somebody in charge had obviously already determined that I was; otherwise, without the imprimatur of a professional, how would I have been permitted to do what I was doing? And so nobody needed to figure out whether I was smart enough or funny enough or nice enough to be worth his interest. Men were interested in me the moment they set eyes on me. This had never happened to me before.

I wish to make it very clear that I was no more attractive than anybody else in the club. If I'd gotten off the bar and put my jeans on, nobody would have given me a second look—an assertion I know to be true because the one time I'd been to

Splash before nobody had given me a second look—and I would have spent the entire evening wishing to be anywhere on the face of the earth but here.

Tonight, however, with my pants off, men were taking it for granted that I was cute and giving me money for it, and in return I was giving them the promise of sex, the promise of *if only*. If only I could get off this bar, if only I didn't have a boyfriend. If only you and I could be together.

And on some level I meant it, just like I had meant it in the tugboat at the party on the pier. The person these men saw had never been asked to leave the floor during the fast skate at the roller rink at Randy Cohen's tenth birthday party because he hadn't been skating fast enough, and Charity Barnett had never told the entire school about it during show-and-tell the next day. The person they saw had never been anything but hot.

Emancipated thus from my crippling past, I was free to interact like a normal human being—to accept what these men offered and to offer what I could in exchange. No, I didn't want to start dating every guy whose hands grazed my ass, but the emotional generosity each one displayed inspired a reciprocal generosity in me. I don't think there was a single guy there I wouldn't have had sex with if circumstances had been different. It wasn't that they were all muscular and sexy; many of them were in fact quite the opposite. But, along with the crumpled bills, they were offering me their own vulnerability. When two gay men meet under potentially romantic but public circumstances, the default dynamic is for each one to appear to want the other less than the other wants him, which is why often people who are dying to sleep together end up not looking at each other for hours at a time. But evidently this rule doesn't apply when one of the two men is a go-go boy, and so these guys were allowing me to see them want me. And I felt deeply honored; I was only sorry to be limited in my recompense to an ass shake or two (or ten, depending on how much they were tipping). How could I not brim with gratitude toward the agents of my liberty?

By the time I staggered out into the street—I had not seen 2:30 A.M. of my own volition since the Clinton presidency—I had made $214 (this number would have been higher, I was told, had patrons not been avoiding Splash after the recent spate of drug busts). It took me three days to recover from the lack of sleep, and after I returned to the land of the living the first thing I did was to e-mail all my friends urging them never to touch singles with their bare hands again, because they had no idea where those bills had been. I left the money I had earned on the coffee table and a few days later, when Mike's parents were visiting us, they asked whether the overflowing plastic cup was my tip jar from tickling the ivories somewhere. The only way I could think of to avoid answering was to pretend to have an embolism, but just as I was about to start faking muscle spasms my dog ran in dragging a stuffed cow, thereby allowing me to effect a graceful change of subject.

But I finally had to face the fact that, fully clothed and standing on the ground, I was once again the timorous, shrinking violet I had been before filling my socks with legal tender. The cup full of wrinkled cash was no match for Samara and Randy and Charity; their power far overshadowed any ephemeral strength lent me by the tender night.

It was obvious that to regain the freedom I had felt so briefly I needed to dance again; luckily, now that I would be performing regularly at Splash, I would be able to feel that freedom weekly. All that remained was for Daniel to tell me to come back, so I waited patiently for his call.

Very patiently.

Very, very *why the fuck isn't the goddamn phone ringing?*

Apparently go-go boys with regular gigs are few and far between, and the rest work freelance. I was horrified to learn this, as it meant that the only way for me to become a fixture in the go-go world—anything less would be a debacle—was either to keep asking party promoters to hire me or to make them love me so much they would move me to the top of their call list. Either proposition would exert enough pressure on me that after three minutes I would turn into a lump of coal.

Nevertheless, I went back to calling and e-mailing and being ignored. Once I even went to Splash on a Saturday and asked the guy running the party whether I could audition for him—watch out, *Feminine Mystique!*—and he said sure.

That night I started to get to know some of the other go-go boys, who were neither haughty nor aloof nor unapproachable but totally friendly. Michael, for example, who had a) no discernible day job but b) the lithest body I had ever seen, won my heart by tipping me even though go-go boys never have to tip one another; I won his in turn by giving him my drink tickets. Later, as we waited offstage to do the shower show (a nightly Splash event in which all the go-go dancers cavort under the water cascading onto them from a mechanism above the stage) he grumbled in frustration at the limited time he had to achieve erection. "Do you have any Viagra?" he asked.

"Wait," I said, "do you have to have a hard-on for this?" I was wearing very well-constructed underwear, so I doubted I would have trouble maintaining the appropriate illusion, but still I was concerned.

"Nah, I just like doing the show better that way." I apologized for not having any Viagra and he turned to Paul, another go-go boy, who was a publicist by day. "Can I use you for inspiration?"

"Sure," came the answer, and Michael reached out and stroked Paul's chest with one hand while working himself to a state in which he could enjoy the shower show with the other. The fourth go-go boy, whose name I never caught, turned out to have the same problem as Michael; Paul helpfully did something interesting to give him the lift he needed, and then it was time for us to go onstage, at which point I found out just how icy cold the showers at Splash really are. A bizarrely nonsexual element pervaded our interactions—these three guys just understood the difficulties inherent in their job, and did what they could to help one another out. As I left the bar, I felt proud to be a member of such a good-hearted group of people, and it took me three days to realize that the guy running the party was never going to call me.

Finally, after weeks of agony, Daniel asked me to help him with a film festival he was organizing and I said yes I would be happy to but *big breath pounding heart shaking voice trembling hands* I wanted him to hire me to dance at Splash as often as he felt comfortable with. He said that would be no problem, and I almost started crying, and then at that week's radio show he told me he'd gotten tired of being micromanaged by the guys who ran Splash so he'd quit.

He hosted a party Saturday nights after the radio show at a bar called Eastern Bloc; I danced there a couple times, but it was nowhere near as satisfying as dancing at Splash. The go-go boys at Eastern Bloc were simply part of the ambience, like the too-loud music and the too-red lights hanging from the too-low ceiling. Nobody paid any attention to us and the tips were terrible. Then one day Daniel said that he was hemorrhaging money and so he was just going to have each week's Eastern Bloc go-go boy do the radio show beforehand as well.

I was being laid off from a job appearing on the radio in my underwear.

I tried not to despair but it was seeming more and more likely that I would never again experience the joy that had filled me during my engagement at Splash. "I'm throwing a party at Scores next Sunday, though," Daniel said (Scores being a notorious heterosexual strip club). "It's the first gay party that's ever happened there. Do you want to help out?" Of course I did. This would undoubtedly turn out to be another defeat to add to my burgeoning store, but the alternative—giving up—was unthinkable.

I assumed I would be dancing, but when I got to Scores and took my pants off I learned that this was not the case. The other go-go boys working the event were going to be dancing—well, technically, they were going to be stripping, the only difference between that and go-go dancing being that they would start this party with their clothes on—but I had a different role to play. Once each go-go boy had finished his featured performance, he would make himself available to interested patrons for lap dances, which was where I came in, as the lap-dance monitor.

My ostensible job was to make sure that none of the patrons and strippers had sex in the lap-dance rooms, but of course my real job was to make sure that the Scores bouncer didn't catch any of the patrons and strippers having sex in the lap-dance rooms. I was also instructed to stop the lap dances after ten minutes, sex or no, so that if a customer was sleazy the go-go boy didn't have to spend too long with him. Shortly after the party started Daniel instructed me to keep anybody who wasn't getting or giving a lap dance from coming upstairs. I wanted to say that I was the least appropriate person within a hundred miles to have been assigned these tasks, since they involved disobeying a burly authority figure, keeping track of time, and telling people "no," but before I could open my mouth he was already gone.

I felt as if I were in a Sartre play. There were sixteen guys at the party in their underwear; fifteen of them were being paid to strip while I made sure everything ran smoothly and helped them out with anything they needed.

I was a go-go intern.

After one go-go boy and his customer left their lap-dance room I opened the curtains to turn the light back on and saw a smear of semen on the leather couch. Though I wanted desperately to pretend I had noticed nothing, I also felt very strongly that the next person to pay for a lap dance in the room had the right to an experience unsullied by the previous patron's ejaculate, so I got a paper towel and, grimacing, wiped the couch clean. I reacted similarly half an hour later in another room when I saw a condom on the floor that had obviously fulfilled its intended purpose. I have taken some unpleasant gigs in the past, but picking up used prophylactics left behind by men who kept having to empty their underwear of cash while I ran frantically around saying "Okay, guys, time to wrap it up" loudly enough to be heard over the patrons' pre-orgasmic groans but not so loudly as to dispel the mood maybe be the worst job I have ever had. When the party was over the go-go boys were supposed to share their tips with me, and every one of them forgot. (One guy did PayPal me the next day but then when I joked that I was shocked he had sex with people he met online he e-mailed me a confused "Why? Doesn't everybody?" and stopped writing me back.) As I was on my way out, Daniel said, "Hey, do you feel like dancing naked at a party tomorrow night?" and, though all I really wanted at this point was to become a eucalyptus plant so I would never be required to have feelings again, I could not summon the psychic resources to turn him down.

A few days after Daniel had first asked me how I felt about dancing naked, remembering what my friend Jim had said about go-go boys dancing with hard-ons, I made an appointment with my primary-care physician. Stuttering with feigned embarrassment, I told Dr. Weinstein that I was suffering from erectile dysfunction caused, I suspected, by my antidepressants. He obligingly wrote me a prescription for Cialis and sent me on my way. And so, the night after the Scores party, I had the appropriate supplies for Daniel's event at Thai One On, a restaurant in the West Village. I knew from Jim and from Go-Go Boy's blog that the evening was likely to be a tawdry one, but beyond that I had no idea what to expect.

"Go-Go Boy says you get paid more if you come," I told Mike as I popped the Cialis on my way out.

"Good," he said, "because the electricity bill was high this month."

I arrived late at the restaurant and found Daniel standing by the clothes check in the vestibule. "The other guys have all already done their sets," he said, pointing to the party room, "so just go on in when you're ready." I couldn't figure out whether I was supposed to be naked here (the people milling about were clothed) or only inside; to be safe, I kept my underpants on until I got into the main room, at which point I realized I didn't know where to store them, so I just threw them in a dark corner and hoped they would still be there when it came time to leave. I got up on a platform wearing only my sneakers and socks, and, following the lead of the other dancers already ensconced in dimly lit niches about the room, manipulated myself into a suitably entertaining condition. I looked up at one point to see Go-Go Boy heading toward me from across the room; I hadn't realized he would be dancing at the party too. "I didn't know you'd graduated," he said affably.

"Yes, well," I replied.

Some of the guests were fully dressed; others were shirtless; still others wore only their underwear. A man in jeans and a button-down shirt came up to me, folded a dollar bill in half, put it in my sock, reached up, and squeezed me a couple times. *Oh, dear,* I thought, *I didn't realize that was part of the deal,* after which I spent half an hour artfully toying with myself in such a way as to prevent anybody else from toying with me. Then I realized that the other dancers, less fastidious than I, were getting much better tips, so I gave over and let the patrons handle the goods (though when one guy made as if to taste them I backed away and laughed in friendly admonishment). Several times during the evening Button-Down-Shirt Man importuned me by repeating the squeezes without the cash incentive. When I rolled my eyes at this, the dancer next to me whispered, "I hate the guys who think a dollar gives them the right to grope you all evening. Just tell him you usually charge a lot more for what he's already gotten." I couldn't figure out how to do this without making Button-Down-Shirt Man dislike me, though, so I held my tongue.

While dressing for the event I had not thought carefully enough, and so instead of long, tight socks I was wearing short, loose ones. This meant that money kept falling out of them, as if I had been blessed by a crone in some twenty-first-century X-rated gay fairy tale. I kept having to collect the bills and put them with my things in the clothes check.

Sometimes guys wanted to talk. One tall fellow with a Vandyke kept coming back to engage me in further conversation, tipping me each time. He asked what I did when I wasn't dancing and I told him I wrote musicals.

"My partner wrote musicals," he said with a rueful smile. "He died a few months ago. You remind me a little bit of him."

I recognized a few people from places I'd danced before. One of them, a shirtless man in his forties with a limp, told me that people never seemed interested in him at these parties and asked me whether I had a boyfriend. I told him I did and he looked around sadly at the room full of flesh and sighed, "All the good ones are taken." I realized he had come here searching for true love and I wanted simultaneously to hug him and to flee.

"Joel!" said another man I had met in my underwear the previous week. "I was hoping I'd get to see you with fewer clothes on." Dave was tall and stocky, with a shaved head and sharp, handsome features. I smiled at him coquettishly, delighted that he had remembered my name.

As the night wore on, the party guests became more adventurous. Every once in a while I would glimpse somebody kneeling in front of somebody else in the shadow of a table, or eventually in the middle of the room, and there were dark figures doing God knows what in the alcove behind me. I became more adventurous too, and lifted myself to hang upside down by my legs from the heavy pipes running across the ceiling. This did not feel as thrillingly Caligulan as I had expected it to, but I was nonetheless gratified by the smattering of applause that greeted my dismount. One of the other dancers, who looked vaguely familiar, urged me not to risk such a maneuver again, in case the pipes weren't strong enough to support me. I bristled at the implication that I was fat but then I realized that the reason he looked familiar was that he had appeared, impressively, in one of my favorite porn movies, so I forgave him the slight.

Finally, at about three-thirty in the morning, I decided it was time to go. What the French call the little death was not required, but after three hours of hard work I would be damned if I was going to leave unfulfilled. Four or five gentlemen were standing around me, including tall and stocky Dave, and, as I accelerated the tempo of the movements in which I was engaged, I made it clear to them through facial expressions and inarticulate noises that I was on the brink of release. I felt a hand on my ass, another couple on my abs, and a few more on various other parts of my anatomy. "Joel's a good boy," Dave said to the man standing next to him, and then looked me in the eyes. "Yeah, he's a good boy."

He cannot have understood the excitatory effect these words would have on me, but they pushed me over the edge. I figured that sound effects would be welcome, so I groaned loudly as I reached the climax of the evening. I am compelled to admit that it was a spectacular example of its species, the kind that leaves one's sides aching as one gasps for air. It took me a minute or two to recover my composure, during which time I saw that the fruits of my labor had landed in a pretty even split between the hands of my assistants and the floor. *I am never going to eat at this restaurant,* I thought as I collected my fee from Daniel. My underwear was nowhere to be found—why I had considered any other possibility I cannot say—so I just put my jeans on, waved goodbye to Go-Go Boy, and left.

Standing outside Thai One On, finding my bearings as the door swung shut, I waited for the familiar feelings of inadequacy, hunger, and need to overwhelm me, waited both to loathe myself until I danced again and to fear that I would never be able to do so no matter how much torture I went through. Putting on clothes at the end of the night had stripped me of any armor against the heartache and the thousand natural shocks that flesh is heir to, and I braced myself.

For something that did not come.

Instead what arrived, unbidden, was the thought *I've gotten what I need to get out of this.* Accompanied by a sense of ease I hadn't felt in years.

As I waited for a taxi amid the noise and bustle of the drunken West Village revels going on around me, I tried to figure out exactly what it was that I'd gotten. Why should tonight have been any different from a night spent dancing at Splash or Eastern Bloc or an afternoon at Scores? Why should I be thinking of Go-Go Boy with equanimity? Why should I picture Samara Zinn and feel the urge to whistle?

I could not find the answer.

I also could not find a cab. At four or so, therefore, I gave up and figured I might as well catch the 3 train. I turned north and, stepping languidly from foot to foot, gyrating at the hip, and sometimes running one hand or the other over my pectoral muscles, headed up Seventh Avenue toward Fourteenth Street.

On Exodus

"You're not the Wicked Witch of the West!" called out the cute, bubbly twink. "You're not going to melt!" I glared at him and stuck my tongue out. "You have until the count of ten and then I'm pushing you. Ten! Nine! Eight! . . ." When Bill got to four I jumped; the log, annoyingly asymmetrical, swung me out over the river, and then I let go and flew through the air, suddenly careless. After I landed I had to swim hard against the current to get to where we had left our things, but when I reached the shore I pulled myself out of the river, climbed back up onto the rock, and did the whole thing again.

I was in North Carolina on the bank of the Asheville River, having accepted Rob's invitation to go swimming. With Rob and me were Louis, Bill, and Greg, all of whom Rob had met that afternoon and all of whom I loathed as soon as they introduced themselves, because Rob might pay more attention to them than to me. Louis, in his forties, was a hairdresser with bad hair; he had checked his voice mail continually during the drive to the river, annoying me more each time. I loathed Bill extra because he was twenty-nine but looked twenty. Greg spoke only in American Sign Language but managed all the same to communicate with supreme hauteur his resentment of me, Louis, and Bill for not letting him have Rob to himself. I had doubtless alienated him further when I introduced myself and misfingerspelled my name as Jopl. I worried about this until "I Will Survive" came on the car radio, at which point I started worrying about the fact that nobody but me could sing along past the first three lines.

I am rarely aware of my physical surroundings. It's an effort for me to walk a city block without bumping into a telephone pole or poking myself in the eye. When we parked by the river and stepped out of the car into the wet air, however, I actually looked through the lenses of my glasses and saw things: the tiny mountains in the distance, the crooked trees across the river, the dark water reflecting the sunlight, the sharp rocks in the dirt under my feet. Then I went to put my contacts in and realized I had forgotten to pour any solution into the case before I left and in the time it had taken us to get here they had become desiccated husks. Since I couldn't very well swim in my glasses, I resigned myself to hoping that I would at least be able to tell the humans from the rocks.

We were obviously not the first people to think of swimming at this spot: a log hung by a rope from a tree on the shore, clearly intended as an aid to swinging out over the river. I scampered after Bill onto the big, flat rock next to the tree; even with my heavily impaired vision I was mesmerized to see that he was wearing what looked like a Victorian bathing costume, one that covered his chest as well as his upper thighs. He chivalrously offered me the log but there was no fucking way I was going first, because what if the river was actually full of piranhas or sulfuric acid?

When Bill dropped into the water, however, he was neither eaten nor dissolved, so I grabbed the log as it swung back— note, please, that this put me *in physical contact with nature*—and watched as Bill climbed out of the river, shaking water from his head like a good-natured dog after a bath.

I couldn't move. I can tread water fine, and I have a passable breaststroke, so it wasn't that I thought I might drown. I was just scared of letting go. And then Bill told me I wasn't the Wicked Witch of the West and started counting.

But I am the Wicked Witch of the West, I thought. When I was five, for my first Hallowe'en trick-or-treating, I had prevailed upon my mother to make me a witch costume, complete with pointy black hat and broomstick; I had run from house to house, swathed in billowing midnight, terrifying all the neighbors with my deep and abiding wickedness and feeling more myself than I ever had before (and, in many ways, than I ever have since).

But this was no time for reverie, as Bill's count was rapidly approaching zero. After my exhilarating jump on "four!" and the subsequent splash I turned around in the water and looked at the Bill-shaped blur on the rock—and the Rob- and Greg-shaped blurs coming toward us, and the Louis-shaped blur sitting on the bank—and realized that I thought of myself in that moment not as a spy and a liar but as a swimmer, and that I thought of the men around me not as ex-gays but as my friends.

In 1976, during a decade that saw any number of wondrous events, a group of sixty-two people gathered in Anaheim, California, to discuss their desire not to be gay anymore. Many of them had already decided to leave what they referred to as "the lifestyle" but were frustrated by the lack of any community or support network. Others had already left the lifestyle and wanted to share with others the truth that such a departure was possible. Still others came simply to meet people like themselves. Evangelical Christians all, they adopted the slogan "Freedom from homosexuality through the power of Jesus Christ," and since then Exodus, International has grown, according to its literature, to include thousands of people on six continents: men and women who, tormented by their homosexual attractions, have joined with God in a struggle to purify themselves by means of something that has become known as "transformational ministry." Though many are still struggling, others have triumphed over what they think of as their sexual brokenness and are now married with children, living lives devoted to the Lord Who has saved them.

Yeah, *right*.

There's no conclusive proof of this, but I think—as does everybody I know—that homosexuality is an inherent trait, like height. If you're short you can wear platform shoes (if you insist), but once you're done growing, that's that. Alter your behavior however you like but you cannot alter your biological makeup. If you are attracted only to people with Adam's apples, nothing is ever going to make your heart leap at the sight of a pair of breasts. Even the comportment of some of Exodus's leaders raises questions about the organization's claims: after a few years, Mike Bussee and Gary Cooper, two of the original sixty-two, left Exodus and their wives for each other. In 2000, John Paulk was removed as board chairman after being photographed leaving a gay bar where he had apparently spent forty minutes trying to pick up another man.

So when my editor suggested that part of my book be about something unexpected and subversive, going undercover among the ex-gays seemed the obvious choice. (What he actually said was "something unexpected and subversive, like you could become a fireman," but unbeknownst to him I had already looked into becoming a fireman, after my boyfriend Mike was late to lunch on the day of the Gay Pride Parade because he had been watching the gay firemen march by, and according to the fire department's website I was *too old* to join the force. I did not share any of this information with my editor because I want him to think of me as vital and young.) When I went to the Exodus, International website I saw an announcement about the thirtieth annual Freedom Conference, to be held in a few months at the LifeWay Ridgecrest Conference Center in North Carolina, so I signed up, sent my check in, and started trying to figure out what to wear.

I had spent my youth in South Carolina, a place teeming with evangelical Christians, so there would be no surprises coming from that direction. But I had never met an ex-gay before. I had never even seen the *Will & Grace* episode in which Neil Patrick Harris tries to get Jack to become an ex-gay. There was an ex-gay who used to hang around at the BGLSA meetings in college, but the only things I can remember about him are that nobody talked to him and that he had really unattractive hair.

As the day of my departure drew near, I wondered more and more what kind of people I would meet at the conference. I couldn't expect them all to be hypocrites. Yes, the examples of Mike Bussee and Gary Cooper and John Paulk led me to suspect that the men and women running the show might not all be exactly what they seemed. But this was a conference for the rank and file; why would hundreds of people gather for a week to lie to no one but one another? It also seemed unlikely that they would all be idiots; the Exodus website was full of eloquent testimonies written by people all over the world. And I doubted they would be simple lunatics; I know mental illness when I see it—I have been dating a psychiatrist for four years—and the registration materials I got in the mail were obviously written by and addressed to individuals in relative control of their mental faculties.

So I woke up the morning of my flight with no inkling of what I was getting myself into. By the time I had to leave for the airport I still hadn't figured out how to dress like an ex-gay, so I just hurled clothing into my suitcase willy-nilly, though thankfully I did have the presence of mind to remove the T-shirt that said I'M NOT POPE BENEDICT XVI BUT MY BOYFRIEND IS before I zipped the bag shut.

"Blessing," said Anne Heche's mother, "is asking God to interfere and bring somebody into the proper relationship with Him."

Nancy Heche was speaking at the opening session of the Freedom Conference as a representative of Parents and Friends of Ex-Gays (PFOX), a group started in 1998 that apparently modeled its title on that of another organization, Parents and Friends of Lesbians and Gays (PFLAG). Her point seemed to be that it was a direct result of her prayers that her daughter Anne had dumped Ellen DeGeneres and become heterosexual (though Nancy did not touch on the causal relationship between her prayers and Anne's claim that as Jesus' half sister Celestia she enjoyed communicating with extraterrestrials). I opened the notebook I had bought to record my impressions of the ex-gays. "LOVE her skirt/blouse combo!!" I scribbled. "So sparkly, looks great w/ green curtain."

Nancy told us that when her husband and her daughter had come out to her she had hardened her heart against them both. "But God spoke to me," she continued. "He said, Nancy, you have to let your heart soften."

There are people in New York to whom God speaks. You meet them on the subway. God tells them all sorts of things, like that the Jews have hidden cameras behind all their mirrors and that the CIA is stealing their thoughts. Often it is a matter of great urgency that they explain these things to you; a matter of far greater urgency in fact than, say, bathing. This happens with enough regularity that New York City has established something called the Homeless Emergency Liaison Project (HELP), which empowers roving teams of psychiatrists to comb the subway for the craziest of the crazies and take them to the hospital and give them large doses of Clozaril.

But as I looked around the nearly full auditorium in North Carolina it was clear that, whatever problems the people in this room had, their solutions did not lie in antipsychotic medication. I learned later that almost a thousand delegates had come to the conference. During the opening session I estimated that three-quarters of the people I saw were men; of these, fully two-thirds were men I would have expected to see at Sunday brunch in Chelsea, waving mimosas and flirting with the waiter. Almost everyone in the room was white, and I saw more moustaches that night than I had encountered in New York in eight years. There seemed to be people of all ages in attendance: A couple of pews to my left sat a man who looked to be in his eighties. Five rows in front of me was a stunning blond in his midtwenties with tantalizingly low-rise jeans and a

YMCA T-shirt worn, I presumed, without irony. But my favorite person so far was the teenager with his hands in his pockets at the end of my row, because his Harry Potter bag had a Slytherin crest on it. "Slytherin kid," I wrote. "May not want be gay, but other priorities = in right place."

Onstage the emcee had taken over for Nancy and was introducing the evening's "worship leader and song receiver," Dennis Jernigan. "Dennis and his wife have been very fruitful and multiplied," she said, "and now they have nine children." This struck me as excessive but then I remembered that I had four cast albums of *The Mystery of Edwin Drood* so I figured I could cut him some slack.

A moustachioed man in his forties walked onstage, sat down at the piano, and began playing soft, inspirational music. "I walked out of homosexuality on November seventh, 1981, at a Christian rock concert," he told us. "The singer said, 'There's someone here hiding something. But God sees it, and He loves you.' I looked around and I thought, well, *you* didn't die for me." Dennis pointed at an invisible person who had neglected to die for him. "And *you* didn't. And *you* didn't. But"—he looked up meaningfully—"He did." As he said this the music he was playing changed from meandering underscoring to what was obviously the introduction to a song. It didn't sound half bad. Then he started singing, in a slightly gruff but pleasant voice.

And it wasn't just a handful of people who stood up and sang with him, not just pockets of Dennis Jernigan enthusiasts scattered throughout the hall. They *all* knew the song, and they all *loved* the song. "Taking my sin, my cross, my shame," Dennis and the standing audience sang, "rising again, I bless Your name." Around me, people lifted their hands in the air, and I saw that people all over the auditorium were doing the same thing, their faces breaking into wide grins. There were a few holdouts—the Slytherin kid was standing but did not smile and kept his hands in his pockets—but before long almost a thousand waving pairs of hands attached to a thousand rapturous open faces reached toward the heavens. I felt as if I were at a Madonna concert in an alternate universe, with an audience full of unstylish people who were not on drugs.

The lyrics to the song Dennis was singing were being projected onto large screens at either side of the stage, against background images of rushing waves and mighty forests and windblown fields of wheat. The words to a verse consistently appeared a line or two after the verse had started. Sometimes they were the words to the wrong verse. At one point the screens read "Rising again, I bless Your nam," which pissed me off. "Spell-check *that* difficult?" I scratched angrily.

But as the song continued I realized that something deeper than bad spelling was at work here. What I saw on the up-turned beaming faces around me was more than just the joy that subsumes people when they get lost in music they love. Yes, that joy was there; but underneath it was a sense of community, of belonging, of acceptance. A man across the aisle from me was sobbing, great, racking gasps of relief, and even the Slytherin kid had started singing along quietly. These people, I thought, spend fifty-one weeks of the year battling homosexual inclinations in isolation. Being here, they must feel like the cavalry has arrived to fight for them and to tell them God is on their side.

Very few Jews I know believe in God as anything but a metaphor. I might not have been able to say this before documents and photographs and film came flooding out of Germany and Poland in 1945, but since then, for many Jews, the only satisfactory answer to the question "What kind of God would allow the slaughter of thirteen million people?" has been "One who doesn't exist."

This perspective had its origins not in the Holocaust, however, but in the nineteenth-century repeal of anti-Jewish laws all over Europe. For millennia, God had been at the center of Jewish life, but as Jews began to mingle in gentile society they felt both less need for the attitudes that marked them as alien and greater hunger for a world beyond the study of Torah. Mainstream Judaism's relationship with God became less intimate, more formal, and many strains of it have stayed that way. For a great number of Jews today, God is Up There somewhere, and the last time He bothered intervening directly on behalf of anybody down here was in Babylon, when He stopped the lions' mouths and delivered His prophet Daniel living from their den. In the Book of Esther, chronologically the next book of Hebrew scripture after Daniel, the name of God never appears. Ever since the eponymous queen saved the Jews from extinction, we may have asked God for any number of things, but a lot of us have seen the requests as purely rhetorical.

Of course this is only one of many Jewish perspectives. There are all sorts of Jews around the world: devout Jews, fundamentalist Jews, mystic Jews, even charismatic Jews. But in America, even if you add them all together, evidently they're still far outnumbered by the Jewish atheists.

And so at the Exodus conference I was deeply unnerved

by all the men and women with their hands in the air; they were reaching up, I realized, absolutely certain that God was reaching down to take their hands and lead them through the wilderness and that, no matter how many times they stumbled, He would keep them from falling. If I believed that, I thought, then I'd probably try to change too, because such wonderful certainty might just be worth it. Unfortunately, I'm pretty much out of luck, because I believe that the Messiah is never coming and that the God of the Jews doesn't hold anybody's hand.

But these people appeared to have come home, and the thought that I didn't belong there was unbearable, because it meant that I had no share in the comfort they felt. So I figured, oh, why the hell not, and raised my hands tentatively, not above my head but to the level of my ears, and burst into tears.

What the fuck? I thought to myself as I sobbed. To this day I don't know whether I was crying because I was feeling what they felt or because I wasn't.

At the First-Timers' Oasis immediately following the opening session I met Jon, who was totally hot and who did not have a moustache. "What brought you here?" he asked, his wife, Stacey, standing mute beside him. "What's going on in your life?" (Stacey had never felt same-sex attractions and was known therefore in Exodus parlance as "everstraight." It had not occurred to me that there would be heterosexual spouses in attendance.) Jon and Stacey, who lived in Los Angeles, had attended their first conference the year before but had come to the First-Timers' Oasis tonight to lend their support to delegates who might be feeling overwhelmed.

"I've been gay for a really long time," I said, beginning the cover story I had carefully prepared before leaving New York, "and there are things about my life I'm dissatisfied with, so I figured I'd come and check it out. I'm actually seeing a guy back in New York, and he knows I'm here, and he's not happy about it. But I felt like I needed to come."

The speech act as a whole was intended to deceive, but by saying only things that were true—there *are* things about my life I am dissatisfied with; for example, the fact that I am not the heir to an oil fortune—I would forestall any compunction.

Jon seemed to accept my explanation. "It's important to realize," he said, smiling broadly, "that *change* is different from *cure.*" A very very handsome man who could easily have appeared in the pages of a calendar a fifteen-year-old wouldn't want his mother to find under his mattress walked by. He waved at Jon and grinned. "That's Matt," said Jon, waving back. "Whatever you've done in the lifestyle, he's done more." *Bitch,* I thought. "He's a firefighter and an EMT. Now, a year ago," said Jon, watching him, "I would have seen him and gone, whew!"—Jon lifted one eyebrow in a picture of lust—"but now I can look at him and think"—his facial expression changed to one of intense concentration, as if maintaining this thought required an Augean effort—"this attraction comes from the fact that I feel inadequate next to him, the fact that I feel less of a man, which I'm not." Stacey's expression did not change and she remained silent as the tomb. I wished for her to disappear so Jon and I could make out, but she did not comply. Very very handsome Matt walked past in the other direction, this time with a friend; both of them were laughing loudly.

I couldn't believe how *happy* so many of these people seemed. I had expected them to be tortured, and instead they were far more at peace than I had ever been in my entire life. They needed but raise their hands in the air to access a comfort I would have sold my soul to feel for five minutes.

What if this was the right choice for them?

The next morning, when I found the site of the imminent "Process of Transformation" workshop, I was filled with dismay. Spending the day with evangelical Christians was one thing; spending the day with evangelical Christians in a low-rent conference room with a dingy carpet and painted cinderblock walls was more than I had signed on for. Unfortunately, however, since my other workshop options were "Understanding the Roots of Lesbianism" and "Parents in Pain: Waiting for the Prodigal," I was pretty much stuck where I was.

On my left sat hot Jon, and on his left sat Rob, whom I had met at the morning session. (There were identically structured sessions every morning and evening, comprising music—Dennis Jernigan was gone, but his replacement for the rest of the week had poorly spelled projections too, so I felt a pleasing sense of continuity—a testimony by somebody who had grown out of homosexuality into the love of Christ, more music, and a sermon.) As I waited now for the Process of Transformation workshop to begin, I resented Rob for pulling hot Jon's focus from me. Jon was a doctor. Rob, who taught high school in a suburb of Cádiz, Spain, was very tall and well built but had a taped-up Bible that had clearly seen a lot of use and was from my home state and dumb.

At the front of the room stood the workshop leader, a middle-aged man named Roy Blankenship who was shaped like a pear and wore the kind of spectacles my brother refers to as child-molester glasses. Roy Blankenship knew from personal experience, he confided to us during the introduction to his PowerPoint presentation, what it felt like to struggle against same-sex attractions. As he began the talk proper I found it difficult to pay close attention, partially because I was thinking about hot Jon but mostly because Roy Blankenship kept putting up slides that said things like "1. When Someone Has Not Yet Been Able To Forgive Either Their Self, Or Others" and it was all I could do not to leap up mid-presentation and copy-edit his visual aids.

I persevered, however, and gained in the end at least a loose grasp of his point, which was, as far as I could tell, that homosexuality is not a naturally occurring phenomenon but the result of childhood trauma or deprivation. "There are three main causes of male homosexuality," Roy said. "There are also fifteen other associated factors, but these three are central. The father wound"—I blinked at this locution but came to understand over the course of the presentation that it referred essentially to a dysfunctional relationship with one's distant father—"rejection by the male peer group, and universal rejection of women because of an intolerable mother, though that last one is rare." In order to start healing, Roy explained, you must first understand how you developed homosexual attractions, which leads in turn to a discovery of what emotional need was never met in your childhood. Once you know what trauma you're compensating for, you can start addressing the *real* problem, which is not homosexuality but insecurity and self-loathing because your father never loved you or you didn't fit in with other boys or your mother smothered you. Then, with continued hard work and a steadfast trust in Jesus, you can begin to heal.

I felt as if I were listening to a lecture by a member of the Flat Earth Society. I heard the phrases coming out of Roy Blankenship's mouth, but my only response was wonderment that an otherwise reasonable-seeming person could string together these combinations of words. I kept thinking, *Did he really just say that?* and realizing that yes, he really had just said that. It occurred to me that perhaps I ought to get angry, but it was impossible to do so, because I found what he was saying less abhorrent than simply nonsensical. I could as easily have taken offense at an argument that gravity is a fraud perpetrated by the Illuminati working in concert with the Freemasons and the Elders of Zion.

Halfway through the presentation, a man resembling a pudgy Dustin Hoffman entered the room; there being no other open seats, I caught his eye and nodded to the chair on my right. Upon sitting down, he immediately began grunting in affirmation of everything Roy Blankenship said.

"When I have a really difficult case in my office," said Roy, "when the person is going on and on about how hard his life is, I reach in and start fiddling in my desk drawer while he's whining, and eventually I say, drat, it's not here. The patient will come out of his self-involvement enough to say something like, what? And I'll say, my magic wand. I can't find it."

"*Yes,*" grunted not-Dustin-Hoffman.

I feel that I would fire Roy Blankenship as my therapist no more than ten minutes into our first session. My problem would be not so much that he believed you can change from gay to straight as that, if you can't be self-involved around your therapist, then what the hell are you paying him for?

But the others in the workshop seemed not to share my concern, and when Roy drew to a close they applauded enthusiastically. As people started to leave the room for lunch, Rob and Jon stayed where they were, deep in conversation with each other. I wanted desperately to join in and make Jon forget that Rob existed and fall in love with me, but if I did so then the grunting man might feel left out, so I started talking to him instead, grinding my teeth whenever Rob laughed at something Jon had said that was obviously funny but that I hadn't quite been able to make out because I had been talking to the grunting man, whose name, he informed me, was Vito.

Vito had been in the lifestyle for twenty-five years and with a man for fifteen of them. When I asked what had led to his change of heart after so long an entrenchment, he said, "I didn't want to die. Eve ate the fruit once. If I go back just once, I could get AIDS. If I die tomorrow I don't want to go to hell—and now I know I'm not going to." I was very brave, he told me; he remembered how difficult it had been for him to take the first step out of the lifestyle. "I railed at God," he said. "Why? Why? I like vanilla, you want me to eat chocolate. Other people have their cake and eat it too. I don't even get to eat the cake. I don't get any cake."

"That's horrible," I said. "I love cake." Vito started honking like a foghorn, in what I had to assume was an expression of enthusiastic concurrence. I wondered whether he was actually mentally ill and then I decided he just had what my psychiatrist boyfriend Mike calls "personality."

"I was at Dennis Jernigan's house," Vito said—*you were where?* I thought—"and I was trying to poke holes in his testimony, and God spoke aloud to me." By this time the idea of a chattering Deity didn't discompose me in the least. "He said, *I told you I'd never leave you, Vito. I didn't tell you it would be easy. Even if no one has ever come out of this lifestyle, I'm calling you out.* I said, Why? Why, God? And He said, *Because I want you to be a light to others. Because of Joel from New York City.*"

I couldn't take this, not even for Rob and hot Jon. I gave Vito a queasy smile and excused myself. When I was on the threshold of the room, he waved at me and shouted, "You're blessed!"

I pointed at him and shouted back, "YOU!"

He pointed at me and shouted, "YOU!"

I shouted, "YOU!," slipped out the door, and went to lunch. There was chocolate cake for dessert but I didn't have any.

I am, under most circumstances, a terrible liar. I've gotten very adept at things like "Yes, honey, I made sure to turn the lights off before we left" and "Of course I paid the cable bill," but when the stakes are any higher than momentary domestic tranquillity I am so overcome with anxiety and guilt that, even if whoever I'm lying to believes me, for hours afterward I am incapable of any activity that doesn't involve thinking obsessively about what a horrible person I am and wondering whether I will get caught.

One would think, then, that attending the Exodus conference undercover might not be the most soothing way for me to spend my time, and Mike suggested as much to me before I left. "By the time you're done you won't be able to sleep anymore," he said. "Ever."

What he failed to understand, however, no matter how hard I tried to explain, was that this would be different. Assuming a persona for a week would be like nothing so much as acting; furthermore, the character I would be playing was virtually identical to the real me, the only difference being that I would pretend an interest in becoming ex gay. None of these people had ever met me, and it was unlikely I would ever see any of them again. How could I feel guilty about wearing a mask in front of people I would know for less than a week? Furthermore, I had no intention of harming those I met or of exposing them in any way—I would be writing about them, certainly, but I wasn't interested in *taking them down*—so what was there to feel guilty about? I was simply doing research, and easy research at that. My plan presented no especial difficulties.

Shockingly, my analysis proved not to have been completely correct. Standing in the auditorium with the Slytherin kid and the YMCA guy and the racking-sobs-of-relief man the night before, what I had felt was not ease but something more akin to nausea. Here was a room full of people reaching with all their might for salvation, and here was me, taking surreptitious notes about their ill-advised tonsorial choices, their bad spelling, and the absurdity of their belief. At the end of the session—as would happen, it turned out, at the end of every session—the worship leader had instructed anybody who wanted to receive a blessing to come up to the front of the room, where a row of well-dressed men and women of varying ages stood at the ready as prayer volunteers. Wanting desperately to receive a blessing, I left my pew and walked twenty feet up the aisle, at which point I turned around and went right back to my seat. I didn't deserve a blessing. Besides, what I really wanted wasn't to be blessed; it was to be forgiven. And such a task was, I suspected, far beyond the powers of a grandfather in a seersucker suit.

So the next day, after Roy Blankenship's presentation, sitting in front of Vito and hearing him say, "Because of Joel from New York City," I felt that nausea even more strongly. One of those absurd people had given me his time, his energy, his attention, because he thought that I was in pain and that he might be able to soothe that pain. How on earth was I to respond to his compassion when my need for it was a lie? I was a two-bit cheat, compelling him to feel honest emotion for me so I could use it in a book about what a fool he was.

After the Exodus conference, when I got back to New York, I figured, okay, if I think this three-main-causes-of-homosexuality-and-fifteen-other-associated-factors stuff is hogwash, why don't I try to find out what's really going on? I had a vague understanding that homosexuality might be genetic—that, for example, male homosexuality could be passed along from mother to son on the X chromosome—but beyond that I knew nothing. When I asked Mike during dinner he said, "Well, we don't really know," so I gave him an extra-tiny scoop of ice cream for dessert and then turned on *Grey's Anatomy,* which he hates, and hid the remote so he couldn't change the channel.

With the help of the Internet, however, I discovered over the ensuing weeks that, though genes certainly play a part in forming future fags, the full picture might be a little more complex than that; the abstract of an analysis of the Australian twin registry by Michael Bailey, Michael Dunne, and Nicholas Martin, for example, suggested an environmental component as well. However, in order to figure out whether "environmental" meant the fetus's environment in the womb—whether different levels of different hormones, for example, could lead to different orientations—or the environment in which the child was raised, I had to read the paper they wrote, and I couldn't understand a goddamn word other than "and" and "the," and I realized that though I had once been smart I was now stupid.

So I gave up and e-mailed Michael Bailey to ask him. He wrote back and said that, though he was certain the environment in question was prenatal, it was at least theoretically possible that the child's social environment in the first year or two of life was involved. The strongest evidence against the latter, he said, comes from the thankfully rare cases in which male babies whose genitalia are either malformed at birth or damaged in accidents are treated by reassignment as females, both socially and surgically. Those babies, genetically male, seem overwhelmingly to grow up to be attracted to women. "How likely is any social explanation of homosexuality," Dr. Bailey wrote, "if you can't make a male attracted to other males by cutting off his penis and rearing him as a girl?"

(He also forwarded my e-mail to a friend of his, who took a look at my website, and then Dr. Bailey forwarded me the e-mail his friend sent him back that said I was cute and funny, so I now have a crush on both Dr. Bailey and Galen Bodenhausen. I have practiced my schoolgirl giggle in case either of them calls me.)

It's always mystified me that the question of whether or not we're born gay winds up at the center of most conflicts about gay rights. If we are, contend gay-rights activists, then we have no control over whom we fall in love with or lust after or blush in the presence of, and it's unfair to punish us for something over which we have no control. If gay people *turn* gay, argue their opponents, then we can just as easily turn straight, and there's no reason to indulge us just because we enjoy being libertines.

The trouble I have with these arguments—aside from their approach to homosexuality as a *problem* that is either *somebody's fault* or *not somebody's fault*—is that whether one has chosen a trait and whether one can change it are two different issues. After talking to Dr. Bailey I tried to think of other human attributes that might illustrate this point, and came up with a grand total of two, food preferences and handedness; I have to congratulate myself, because it turns out that we are born with our taste preferences and yet they can change over time—most people are born hating cilantro, for example, but many grow to enjoy it over time—and that handedness, though usually partially determined by early social environment, is subsequently immutable—the only thing tying a lefty's dominant hand behind his back accomplishes is to traumatize him and give him a stutter. (None of the experts I talked to about these things called me cute or funny, so I don't remember their names.)

Who's to say, then, that if we're born gay we can't change, or that if we become gay after birth we can? (The question usually left unasked is: if gay people can become straight, *so fucking what?* Quakers can become Methodists too, but you don't see anybody rushing to pass laws to prevent members of the insidious Society of Friends from marrying one another.)

So I don't think the question of whether we're born gay is all that compelling. To me, the more interesting question is: how effective are attempts to change sexual orientation?

In recent years, I discovered after exhaustive research involving Google and a pint of Häagen-Dazs chocolate peanut butter ice cream, there have been only two relevant studies, and though they were held up in the media as yielding conflicting results, as far as I can tell they fit together pretty well. Robert Spitzer, who spearheaded the successful effort in the 1970s to remove homosexuality from the American Psychiatric Association's list of mental illnesses, interviewed 200 people recommended to him by ex-gay ministries and concluded that "some highly motivated individuals" can change their orientation, but that such instances are "rare" and that "the vast majority of gay people would be unable to alter by much a firmly established homosexual orientation." Ariel Shidlo and Michael Schroeder, after talking to 202 people who had undergone therapy to try to become straight, determined that 4 percent of them had successfully changed their sexual orientation but that 77 percent of them had suffered "significant harm" as a result of the therapy.

Of course both studies left room for doubt. Dr. Spitzer had talked only once with each subject, whereas Dr. Shidlo and Dr. Schroeder conducted follow-up interviews in which some subjects recanted their previous statements. But Shidlo and Schroeder's study presented uncertainties too. Just as Spitzer recruited his subjects through Exodus and other ex-gay organizations, Shidlo and Schroeder recruited many of theirs from LGBT publications; in the early days of the study they had even asked specifically for people who felt they had been harmed by "homophobic therapies," though they changed the wording of their advertisements before long. Furthermore, both studies assessed sexual orientation by interview rather than by physical testing. It's easy to lie with words, to others and to yourself. When there's an electronic monitor checking to see whether you get an erection while watching *Mount Fuck-*

more, however, deception might become a little more difficult to maintain.

On top of all that, none of this research takes bisexuality into account. According to the sex researcher of all sex researchers, Alfred Kinsey, human sexual experience covers a spectrum—people who have never had any homosexual fantasies or encounters are a zero on the Kinsey scale, people who have been exclusively homosexual are a six, and people who have had various amounts of experience with both sexes fall somewhere in between the two.

(That's one thing this conference did for me: I now believe in male bisexuals. Women's sexuality seems to be capable of a great deal of fluidity, but I was always certain, like most gay men, that guys who claim to be bisexual are either deluded or lying. At the Exodus conference, however, I met a surprising number of people whom I really believed when they said they enjoyed both heterosexual and homosexual sex, and I began to reconsider my position. The men I spoke to may not have relished sex with women as much as they relished sex with men—which, according to Dr. Bailey, is consistent with data suggesting that psychological bisexual arousal is more common than physical bisexual arousal—but the next time somebody tells me he likes boys and girls I will not automatically assume he is on the bi-now-gay-later plan.)

My take on Spitzer, Shidlo, and Schroeder is that the 4 percent of highly motivated individuals who changed had probably fallen somewhere in the middle of the Kinsey scale and simply reinforced some attractions while ignoring others.

Or maybe they were fooling themselves.

Or maybe they were lying.

Or maybe they really had turned straight.

Who the fuck knows? I believe that fundamental change

of this sort is impossible. But I also once believed that if you swallowed chewing gum it would get caught in the little hammers in your esophagus that pulverized food as it went down and the little hammers would get gunked up and stop working and you would be unable to digest food and you would starve to death. So I can imagine, at least theoretically, the rare case in which a person who honestly identifies as gay becomes a person who honestly identifies as straight.

What I cannot imagine is that this father-wound-rejection-by-male-peer-group-rising-again-I-bless-Your-nam crap is the way to go about it.

Further inquiry led me to Wikipedia—my God, to think that people used to have to *go to the library*—where I learned that Exodus's transformational-ministry approach is a religious variation on something called "reparative therapy," which was invented in the middle of the twentieth century by three psychiatrists (working independently) named Edmund Bergler, Irving Bieber, and Charles Socarides. They are no longer with us but their work has been continued by counselors such as Joseph Nicolosi (president of the National Association for the Research and Treatment of Homosexuality), Gerard van den Aardweg (author of *The Battle for Normality*), Richard Cohen (director of the International Healing Foundation), Jeffrey Satinover (author of *Homosexuality and the Politics of Truth*), and David Matheson (co-creator of the Journey Into Manhood experiential-weekend program). Their approaches differ from one another to a greater or lesser degree, but are generally all aimed at helping the little boy within free himself of neurotic homosexual attractions by becoming a man.

My problem with the work I was reading about wasn't that I found its goals objectionable, though I did; my problem was that its authors were about as rigorous in their approaches as kindergarten music teachers. Most of the evidence supporting reparative therapy's efficacy came in the form of anecdotal studies therapists had written about their own patients, studies that had never been independently verified. Taken as a whole, the reparative approach seemed to lack any consistent standard of care. There was no consensus on what constituted successful treatment (heterosexual desire? lack of homosexual desire? abstinence from homosexual sex regardless of desire? complete celibacy? attending a monster-truck show?). Nobody had satisfactorily addressed the increasingly prevalent idea that women's sexual orientation behaves differently from men's. The links reparative therapists made between cause and effect, both in the origins of homosexuality and in its treatment, were as far as I could tell only theories spun by men who talked a good game but who didn't back themselves up with anything solid. (In a version of *A Parents' Guide to Preventing Homosexuality* quoted on the Focus on the Family website, for example, Nicolosi wrote that a father who wishes to prevent his son from becoming gay "can play rough-and-tumble games with [him], in ways that are decidedly different from those he would play with a little girl . . . help his son learn to throw and catch a ball . . . teach him to pound a square wooden peg into a square hole in a pegboard . . . [and] even take his son with him into the shower, where the boy cannot help but notice that Dad has a penis, just like his, only bigger.")

I don't care how many books Nicolosi and friends publish about their own success in the treatment of same-sex attraction. When they do a truly meticulous study, with double blinds and controls and a random sampling and minimal theoretical and procedural weaknesses, vetted by other professionals in the field, that points to an explicit causal link between an absent father and a gay son, or between holding therapy and reduced same-sex erotic fantasizing—*then* I'll start taking them seriously.

(After this book went into production, Stanton Jones and Mark Yarhouse published a third study, which, while it shares some of the fundamental flaws of the other two, appears in many ways to be more rigorous. The study is 406 pages long and contains approximately a googolplex tables and charts, and I am not a statistician; that said, I interpret it as suggesting a 5 percent success rate for conversion therapy. Watch somebody come up with an analysis of the study that proves me completely wrong and publish it the day after I've sent the proofs back to my editor.)

But if I have to choose between my gut feeling, which seems to be supported by what little data we have, and Power-Point slides that say "When Someone Has Not Yet Been Able to Forgive Either Their Self, Or Others"—well, I know which side I'm coming down on.

If there had been any doubt I had returned to the South, it would have been dispelled by the menu at the LifeWay Ridge-crest cafeteria. On offer for dinner the day of "The Process of Transformation," for example, was chicken-fried steak, ham and hash-brown casserole, and fruit salad with maraschino cherries and mini-marshmallows, which by the way was irresistible despite being *so* not allowed on the South Beach Diet. To drink we had a choice, as at every meal, between fruit punch, which I avoided because it was blue, and chocolate milk. (When I left my agent and my editor clandestine messages later that night to let them know I was okay I went on and on about the fruit salad, but I was speaking as quietly as possible so as to avoid detection, and later they told me that all they had heard was incomprehensible whispering punctuated occasionally by the word "mini-marshmallows.")

Hot Jon, sitting across from me at dinner, was drinking the fruit punch as he talked to me about his path to Exodus. "When I was a kid," he said, "I was molested by a male scout-master and a female babysitter." In high school, he continued, he had told his mother that he had feelings for other boys. She found him a counselor who claimed to be able to change these feelings; after working with him for a while, Jon felt he'd licked his problem. Unfortunately, a few months after he and Stacey got engaged, his massage therapist had started becoming suggestive during their weekly sessions. "Eventually he went for it," Jon said, "and I was like, *no!* I told Stacey about it, and she understood." They had gotten married and things were fine, except that Jon found himself looking more and more at gay porn. "Then I was at a medical conference," he said, "and I acted out with another guy." *Wait,* I thought, *you did **what** with another guy?* "It was awful. I told Stacey, and we decided to come to the Exodus conference." What must it be like, I wondered, to have to tell your wife that other men excite you in ways she never has and never will? I can barely bring myself to tell my boyfriend I ate all the Corn Pops.

When his tale came to a resting place, Jon asked me to tell him more about myself; I repeated my cover story from the night before with a few more adjectives thrown in.

"But *what* do you feel dissatisfied with?" he said.

I realized with a lurch that my spiel, while sufficient for brief interactions, was useless here; I hadn't counted on the fact that information is currency. Jon had told me a revealing story about himself, and in return I was obliged to tell him an equally revealing story about myself. To do otherwise would have been taking something without paying for it: not just impolite but hostile.

Yet I had prepared nothing beyond my painstakingly crafted three sentences, so I had no idea what to say. I inhaled, about to speak, and then I heard Rob's voice behind me saying, "Guys, I have to tell you about the workshop I just went to." He kept talking and I breathed a sigh of relief, because God only knows what would have come out of my mouth once my vocal cords had started vibrating.

Acted out. Struggler. Father wound. Broken. The lifestyle. Words became amorphous at the conference, taking on shades of euphemism they do not ordinarily enjoy in New York. The whole time I was in Asheville, I don't think I heard one person utter the phrase "have sex with"; instead, everybody said "acted out," which, I realized eventually, could mean anything from "fucked" to "masturbated" to "stole my ex-boyfriend's Carmen Miranda hat and then wore it to his Oscar party where I deliberately spilled Cabernet on his Louis Vuitton jacket." "In the lifestyle" meant that somebody identified as gay. "Ministry" meant trying to convince gay people to become ex-gay.

Much of the Exodus vocabulary was infused with a sense of poetry. A person trying to overcome same-sex attractions was a "struggler." Singing was "worship." To be imperfect or traumatized was to be "broken." Once words were separated thus from their meanings, it seemed to me, they could be used to mask otherwise unpalatable ideas. I would react violently against the idea of trying to become straight, but who wouldn't leap at the chance not to be broken anymore?

"There is no such thing as a homosexual person," I heard over and over again during the conference. "There is only a heterosexual person with a same-sex attraction problem." Vito's bit about chocolate vs. vanilla cake was clearly part of a great tradition of sugary-snacks metaphors. I think five different people explained to me that gay sex was like ice cream. "When you're hungry," said Jon, "you can decide to have a banana split, but other things are much better for you." "You have to catch yourself *before* you're on the verge of acting out," said somebody else. "If the ice-cream cone is in your hand, there's no way you're not going to start licking it." I found these arguments unpersuasive, because I believe it's actually very important to eat sugary snacks; it reminds us of what we all have in common. There's something about opening a pack of M&M's, for example, that makes me feel connected to the world. Whether I eat them individually or by the handful, whether I separate all the green ones out or not, I am sharing a simple pleasure with every creature on earth possessed of taste buds.

Of course, the Exodus community is not the only one with its shibboleths. Show me a homosexual man who can't complete the sentence "Life's a banquet, and most poor suckers are _____," and I'll show you a homosexual man who was raised by wolves. (The answer, in case you are a homosexual man who was raised by wolves, is "starving to death." Now put this book down, go rent *Auntie Mame,* and don't start reading again until you've watched it at least six times.)

After dinner with Jon I stopped at the LifeWay Christian Store. This was not my first visit to an evangelical bookseller; when I was in eighth grade, as an exercise in sociological observation, my family had spent a weekend at Heritage, USA, the theme park created by televangelists Jim and Tammy Faye Bakker. Everybody there said please and thank you all the time, the ceiling of the mall was painted sky blue so you felt like you were outside, and the Tammy Faye Bakkery (would that I were joking) sold really good cookies. When I found the music store I was very excited until they told me that not only didn't they have Heart's new album (*Bad Animals*) but they had never even heard of Heart. The bookstore, fortunately, yielded better results. True, they didn't carry *Magician's Gambit* (the sequel to *Queen of Sorcery*, which I had finished in the car on the way up, and I was going *crazy* not knowing what Eternal Belgarath and Prince Kheldar had been up to while Polgara the sorceress had been rescuing Garion from the palace of Salmissra the Serpent Queen), but they offered a number of other fascinating books, each one more outré than the last; I finally selected a slim volume called *Satan's Mark Exposed,* about how bar codes are instruments of the devil, because the guys in one of the sketched illustrations were really cute.

The tables in the LifeWay Christian Store were piled high with soothing titles like *He, Watching Over Israel* and *Worthy Is the Lamb,* but farther toward the back I was thrilled to find *Satan's Mark Exposed.* My copy had long since gone the way of all flesh, and I was delighted to have the opportunity to replace it. As I skimmed the familiar lines, however ("By way of electronics, Antichrist will be able to invade the privacy of your home as you have devotions! In the Tribulation Period Christians will suffer persecution and have nowhere to hide! The day will soon come when all hospitals will refuse admittance to a

mother with a sick child because neither bears the Mark of Antichrist!"), I was distracted by the bubbling of three teenagers
looking at bracelets.

"*Totally* get the FROG one," said a dark-haired boy wearing a "What Would Jesus Do?" T-shirt.

"FROG?" said the blond boy beside him.

"Um, Fully Rely On God," said the girl.

"I want this one," said the blond.

"Um, the rainbow one?"

"Don't get that one." Scorn filled the dark-haired boy's
voice. "People will *totally* think you're *gay.*"

I wanted to yell at them for being uncharitable at a Christian
conference center. I also wanted to hide so they didn't see me.
Not that I really thought they would beat me up among shelves
of inspirational literature, but still I was afraid; of exactly what,
I couldn't say. I stepped behind a display rack and, ashamed of
my cowardice, turned my Exodus conference name tag around
so it didn't face out. I bought a notebook (I'd filled up the old
one) with characters from something called Veggie Tales on the
cover—I was at a loss to say what a cucumber, an asparagus, and
two unidentifiable vegetables, all dressed as gangstas, had to do
with Jesus—and left, making sure to take the path that kept me
farthest away from the teenagers. The ex-gays may be delu-
sional, I thought as I made my way back to my room, but they're
better Christians than a lot of people we call sane.

Before leaving New York I had decided to bring along
episodes of television shows on DVD, in case of sleeplessness

or suicidal ideation. I had searched Kim's Video for *Oz*, HBO's violence- and gay-sex-filled prison drama, but somebody had checked out the seasons with Chris Meloni *(naked* Chris Meloni, to be precise), so I picked up the 1980s version of *The Twilight Zone* instead.

Back in my room after my visit to the LifeWay Christian Store, in an effort to regain the equilibrium that had vanished with the real-world homophobia I had just witnessed, I put the first *Twilight Zone* DVD in my computer. I was hoping for the feel-good episode in which a present-day teenager saves an eighteenth-century girl from execution as a witch, but instead the first episode, entitled "Shatterday," began with Bruce Willis (oh, my God, he has hair!) as an asshole in a bar who picks up the phone (oh, my God, it's a rotary dial!) and accidentally calls his own home, where the phone is answered by Bruce Willis. The two Bruce Willises spend the rest of the week dueling over one life; in the end the kinder, more responsible one triumphs, and the selfish and inconsiderate Bruce fades into nothingness. I hated the new Bruce for being perfect when the old Bruce was defective like me.

But that's what the Exodus delegates are after, I thought. They want their imperfect selves to fade into nothingness and be replaced by new, flawless Bruce Willises with upturned collars and feathered hair.

In *Man of La Mancha,* the Wasserman-Leigh-Darion musical based on Miguel de Cervantes's *Don Quixote,* Cervantes tells his antagonist, "When life itself seems lunatic, who knows where madness lies? Perhaps to be too practical is madness. To surrender dreams—this may be madness. To seek treasure where there is only trash. Too much sanity may be madness. And maddest of all, to see life as it is and not as it should be." Cervantes speaks these words in prison, knowing that within the hour, in all likelihood, the flames of the Inquisition will be licking at his calves.

So what are the ex-gays doing but seeing life not as it is but as they think it should be, even as they hear the kindling begin to crackle? They are fools and heroes wrapped up together, straining with all their might to change something unchangeable. They are trying to rid themselves of something they see as immoral and pathological and unholy, and from that perspective, I believe, they are among the noblest people on earth. If a serial rapist—to make a fraught comparison—were to struggle with all his heart and all his soul and all his might against the inclinations that impelled him to violate others, if he were to go to therapy and church and hope and beg and pray to be relieved of his desires, I would laud his efforts and support him as best I could, even as I grieved that the continued urge to rape, studies indicate, is not something that can be gotten rid of. Serial rape has nothing to do with homosexuality, but if I lived, like the ex-gays, in a universe in which the two were morally equivalent, I would be sitting right now astride my ragged, scarred horse, spear in hand, galloping toward the windmills.

The statuesque figure of the speaker at the next morning's session made it difficult for me to believe that she was not in fact a drag queen. Kathy Koch (author of *Finding Authentic Hope and Wholeness*) told us that her sermon was called "Mordecai and Esther: Teamwork to Transform," which I was excited to learn, as Mordecai and Esther are characters at the center of the fabulous Jewish holiday Purim.

"Purim" is the Hebrew word for "lots," referring in this case not to a selection system based on chance but to a combination of math, logic, and astrology used long ago to schedule important events (weddings, coronations, the slaughter of all the Jews in Persia). The bare bones of the Purim story are as follows:

In the city of Shushan, Mordecai the Jew refused to bow down to the wicked vizier Haman, and so in retaliation Haman convinced the king to order the extermination of the Jews on the date he had selected by lot. But Mordecai had an ace up his sleeve: his cousin Esther happened to be married to the king. She had thus far neglected to mention to her husband that she was a Jewess, but in her people's time of need she revealed her secret to him and begged him to save them. The king could not rescind an order he had already given, but he issued a new decree that the Jews be allowed to arm and defend themselves, which they did, to great effect, and at the end of the day Haman swung from the gallows he had erected for Mordecai.

Kathy Koch, alas, gave an insipid sermon, explaining merely that we all need to be both Mordecai and Esther. We need to Mordecai—she actually turned the name into a verb— by *instructing* and by *remaining present.* And we need to Esther by *choosing a Mordecai,* someone who will instruct us and remain present in our lives for a long time.

Purim is my favorite Jewish holiday. We celebrate our deliverance by dressing in costumes and putting on masks. We read the Book of Esther in synagogue and whenever Haman is mentioned we boo and shake noisemakers and overpower the sound so as to blot out his memory under heaven; every time

Swish

Kathy Koch said "Haman" I had to resist the impulse to hiss and stamp. On Purim it is considered a mitzvah—a commandment, a good deed—for us to enfeeble our evil inclinations by getting so drunk we can't tell the difference between "blessed be Mordecai" and "cursed be Haman." (The last time I fulfilled this mitzvah I slammed my hand down next to my plate in the middle of dinner with friends and slurred, "I'm smarter than everybody at this table put together!" Since then on Purim I have stuck with Diet Mountain Dew.) Purim is the only holiday that will still be celebrated after the coming of the Messiah.

There are innumerable explanations for the custom of masks, all of which explanations pretty much work together. For example: we pretend to be other people to represent a world turned upside down, a world in which Haman can decree the murder of the Jews one day and perish along with his wife and children the next. And/or: we assume different faces so as to understand that true reality and the reality we perceive may be different things. But my favorite interpretation is that we don physical masks in order to cast off the psychic masks we wear every other day of the year. If we put on a face that we acknowledge as false, then underneath it we can liberate our true selves.

The Hebrew name for the Book of Esther is *Megillat Esther,* which can be taken, I believe, to mean "to reveal what is hidden." The fact that God's name never appears in the Book of Esther is to be understood, say the sages, as an indication that, though His hand is invisible—hidden—His work is revealed everywhere.

Purim is a holiday of secrets, of masks, of divided selves, of mystery, of revelation. What better topic for a sermon at the ex-gay conference?

But that's not what Kathy Koch chose to talk about.

If I had any inclination to believe there was anybody up there watching out for us, nudging us in this direction or that at moments in which our choices could bring us to happiness or to despair, I would find powerful support in what happened later that day. Expecting the evening session to be just as tedious as all the other sessions, I had resolved to skip it, yet I found my steps taking me not back to my room to watch more of *The All-New Twilight Zone* but to the auditorium. Had I followed my original impulse, I would not have been present at one of the most extraordinary events it has ever been my privilege to witness.

I would have missed the ex-gay musical.

Acts of Renewal, according to the emcee, was a theater troupe led by Mr. and Mrs. Jim Shores, both instructors at North Carolina's Montreat College. He taught students in the Environmental Studies Department, with a focus on marine biology; she taught in the Worship Arts Department. Acts of Renewal had been performing original theatrical entertainments around the country for over a decade, but they had chosen to wait for the Exodus conference to premiere their first musical, *The Promised Land*.

The action of *The Promised Land* concerned four people who had decided not to accompany Joshua into Canaan with the rest of the People Israel because they found crossing the River Jordan inconvenient. There were two women, a Lesbian and a Woman Who Judged Her Husband for Engaging in Homosexual Behavior, and two men, a Fag and a Seemingly Respectable Man Who Proved Later to Have a Distasteful Secret Involving Anonymous Sex in Dangerous Parts of Town (these are my own designations for the characters; their actual names were Jered, Hannah, Zerubebel, and Tiffany). As the lights went up, the Seemingly Respectable Man Who Proved Later to Have a Distasteful Secret Involving Anonymous Sex in Dangerous Parts of Town suggested to the other three that they all consider crossing the Jordan that night; they responded by singing a song from *West Side Story*, but instead of "Tonight, tonight/Won't be just any night,/Tonight there will be no morning star," they sang "Not tonight, not tonight,/We cannot cross tonight,/Tonight is just a bad time for me." The Lesbian couldn't cross, she sang, because she had to call her girlfriend; the Fag was going to frost his hair; they all needed at least six more weeks of counseling. They brought the number to a rousing finish ("With work and therapy, I'll get it right,/Just not tonight!") and then, as the Seemingly Respectable Man Who Proved Later to Have a Distasteful Secret Involving Anonymous Sex in Dangerous Parts of Town stood dumbfounded, the three other members of Acts of Renewal made what may have been the most brilliant transition ever conceived in the musical theater and broke into, "Tomorrow! Tomorrow!/We'll cross it tomorrow!/It's only a day away!"

I stared agape, my mind unable to compass the number of ways in which this was so very, very wrong.

The show went on for half an hour and included ex-gay versions of songs such as "Too Darn Hot," "Cry Me a River," "They Call the Wind Maria" ("They Call My Sin Desire"), and "Diamonds Are a Girl's Best Friend" ("Biceps Are a Boy's Best Friend"). The musical-theater writer in me grew more and more perturbed to see Acts of Renewal take such brazen liberties with other people's intellectual property; of course I had no certain knowledge of this, but I found it impossible to imagine that they had gotten permission from the writers of these songs to change their words, especially not Stephen

Sondheim (gay), Frederick Loewe (gay and dead), and Cole Porter (gay, dead, and bitchy).

As the performance drew to a close, the characters saw God wading across the Jordan toward them, and, singing a stirring finale, stepped into the river to meet Him halfway. The curtain calls lasted for a very long time.

During the applause I found myself thinking of the late seventeenth and early eighteenth centuries, when Baroque music reached its zenith in the persons of Handel, Porpora, and their contemporaries. All important opera roles were sung by sopranos and mezzo-sopranos, some of them women, some castrated men. Both women and men sang male and female roles; the audience didn't care as long as the voices they heard were thrilling. Furthermore, opera plots could be more complicated than that of any Ludlum thriller, so it was entirely possible to have, say, a male singer playing the part of a woman whose character has disguised herself as a man to rescue her male lover, played by a woman, from captivity at the hands of a sorceress, played by a man.

Baroque opera had nothing on Acts of Renewal.

Two gay men claiming to have become straight men were playing the parts of two gay men in an attempt, via a medium strongly associated with gay men, to convince an audience of gay men and lesbians to become straight men and straight women; they were aided in their efforts by 1) a lesbian who claimed to have become a straight woman, playing the part of a lesbian and 2) the everstraight wife of one of the two gay men.

The members of Acts of Renewal did not have the acting chops to pull this off convincingly.

To my dismay, on my way into the Men's Panel discussion before lunch the next day I ran into Rob, the dumb high school teacher from Cádiz. If he sat next to me my ability to take notes would be severely hampered, but in the end I was too slow-witted to escape his company.

In an uncomfortable attempt to make conversation before the panel started, I asked him how he had made his way from South Carolina to Spain. He proceeded to tell me a dizzying story of military service and international travel and degrees at institutions of higher learning. The more he talked the more I suspected he might not actually be dumb. As an officer in the navy, he told me, he had started studying American Sign Language; eventually he became fluent and, after teaching math at a school for the deaf, got a job as an ASL interpreter. He joined a deaf church, where he participated in the van ministry (I had a wild image of Rob trying to save the souls of the deaf church's SUVs but then I realized he meant he'd just ferried the churchgoers to and from the services). I kept waiting for him to say something that would indicate some lack of generosity or other-directedness somewhere, but I waited in vain.

Then the panel began, interrupting our conversation, and it was just too dreary for words. There were five men on it, all of whom had the same kind of story as everybody else here: they had been molested, they had had terrible relationships with their fathers, they had gotten married, they had cheated on their wives, they had joined the gay community, they had left the gay community. Two of the panelists had excellent highlights (the whole time I was at the conference I didn't see a single person with bad highlights). Nobody said anything in the panel discussion that I hadn't heard before: brokenness, molestation, struggler, peer rejection, father wound. One of the men with highlights said he had decided to leave the lifestyle after he had been having sex with another man and Jesus had appeared at the foot of his bed. "I'll go wherever you go," Jesus had apparently announced, which I thought was the best setup ever for a scene from a porn movie, but that turned out not to be how the encounter had progressed.

As the panel broke up and people headed for lunch, Rob asked me why I was taking so many notes. Terrified he would find me out, I began to stutter: "Um, I, uh, I want to be able to look at this four months from now, um, and say, 'Oh, my GOD, *that's* what he meant!'" As soon as I said "GOD" I regretted taking the Lord's name in vain at the ex-gay conference, but Rob didn't seem to mind.

"I don't understand your struggle," he said. "I mean, you just up and came here?"

After my near miss with Jon ("But *what* are you dissatisfied with?") I was prepared for this. I gave Rob facts that were true, but I made specious connections between them. "I've just been a real asshole to people," I said, "cheating on my boyfriend, treating him like dirt. And I want not to be like that anymore. I want to be a better person, but it's hard to find support for that in the lifestyle. So I figured I'd come here and see what I could learn." I had cheated on my boyfriend and treated him like dirt, true, but that had been years ago, before we were officially boyfriends. Now we were so boringly faithful we might as well have been living in Levittown.

I was beginning to feel uneasy, though, so to deflect Rob's curiosity I started asking him questions about himself. He had acted out, he said, in April, when, while on vacation in Boston, he'd learned that his mother had been diagnosed with leukemia. "I just wanted someone to hold me," he said. "The strugglers I knew in Boston didn't answer their phone. I knew where the cruising spots were, so I picked up a guy at a rest stop and went back to his apartment. I didn't really want to do anything, but I couldn't say no. I couldn't stop myself. We did stuff I'd never done before. The only things about homosexual sex I can't stomach are oral sex and anal sex. I've never done anal, but that night I had oral sex, and it was no good. It didn't make any sense. Where was the emotional connection?" I was so caught up in trying to figure out what was left if you ruled out oral and anal sex that I couldn't answer the question. "The next night I talked to two strugglers about it and they were terrific. At the end of the conversation we had a big group bear hug. It felt good and right, not like the night before." I noticed a touch of gray in Rob's circle beard and sideburns, and in the tufts of hair showing between the parted collar of his shirt. I realized with a start that he was actually incredibly hot.

"What was it like in the military?" I asked. Rob started talking about traveling and radio software and safeguarding command codes and completely ignored my real question, which was, In the military was there lots of hot gay sex?

"So somebody could have captured you and tortured you for the command codes?" I asked.

"Only if they tickled me." Oh, my God, he was *flirting* with me!

As we left the now-empty room, Rob suggested I come visit him in Cádiz. "You'd really like some of my international friends," he said. I thought, *I could totally have him if I wanted.*

My attempt to eat dinner alone that evening so I could take notes in my notebook with the gangsta cucumber and the gangsta asparagus and the two unidentifiable gangsta vegetables on it was foiled by the appearance of a stocky dark-haired man who exclaimed, as he sat down across from me, "Veggie Tales *rocks!*" Such an opener did not incline me to conversation with him, but I was trapped.

When in our introductory exchanges I mentioned to David that I was Jewish, he said, "Me, too!" I raised my eyebrows, amazed to find another Jew here. "Well, actually, I'm . . . let's see . . . how should I . . ." *Oh, no,* I thought. *No. Anything but*—"I'm a Jewish person who believes."

He was a fucking Jew for Jesus.

It can be difficult for gentiles to understand why Jews tend to loathe the Jews for Jesus more than we loathe anything else upon the earth, including neo-Nazis and going camping.

But imagine that you're one of the Chosen People, and that your identity is based on the idea that you have a unique relationship with God. For thousands of years your people has been persecuted for being different; you could have changed that at any point by accepting Jesus, but you didn't, because it would have meant giving up that relationship with God, and if inquisitions and pogroms and genocide have been the price you've had to pay, then so be it.

Now imagine that along come these folks who say, We get the unique relationship with God *but we also get to be just like everybody else!* We can enjoy the cachet of being different and relax in the comfort of the majority at the same time! We get to have our cake and eat it too! We get to be the Chosen People *and not pay for it!*

What are you going to think? You're going to think that it's a cheat, an outrage, an insult to human decency and to every Jew who has ever been slaughtered for refusing to bow to a graven image.

So when David revealed himself to me as a Jew for Jesus, my first impulse was to spit in his face. "I don't understand that," I said finally, and realized immediately how rude it sounded. "I mean, can you explain that to me?" Hardly better. "I just mean . . . not *make me understand* but *talk to me more about it.*" *Please, God,* I prayed, *help me not commit murder here in the Life-Way Ridgecrest cafeteria.*

"The short answer," he said, "is that I was absolutely pierced in the heart by Christian friends who convinced me." *Some friends,* I thought. "The long answer is that I was just unfulfilled by Judaism. I just felt something was missing. And as I started to look at Christianity, I felt like, well, okay, either Jesus was a liar and a lunatic, or he was the real thing. And too many people believe in him for him to have been a liar and a lunatic. So I realized he had to be real."

"Can I ask you a question?" I said. "Do you consider yourself Jewish—"

"Yes."

I gritted my teeth at the interruption. "—or Christian?"

"Yes." I was a hair's breadth away from slapping him. "I'm still one of the Chosen People. My Christian friends love that I'm a Jew who has come to the faith. I'm just glad I'm not bound for eternal hell."

I wasn't going to touch that one. "All right," I said. "Here's another question. People here keep saying things like 'I trust God's plan for me' and 'God supplies all my needs.'" David nodded. "So take Darfur, where half a million people have been massacred by the Janjaweed militia. Has God been supplying their needs? And if not, why not?"

This is what drives me crazy whenever I hear people say things like, "Ask the universe for what you want, and you'll get it," why I fucking *hated* that Paulo Coelho book *The*

Alchemist that everybody was reading in the late nineties. Whenever I saw the book in anybody's hands on the subway I always wanted to say, "So the reason a million Tutsis were just slaughtered in Rwanda is that *they didn't ask the universe not to kill them?*"

It was obvious as soon as David opened his mouth that he had never thought about such a question before. He kept talking and talking about how our only real need is to be in line with God's will and He's a jealous God and blah blah blah blah blah and I stopped listening and started toying with my spoon, wishing I could plunge it into his eye sockets and pop out his eyes. What I really wanted was to take an ancient Egyptian brain hook (a mummification tool), shove it up his nose, and yank his brains out through his nostrils, but all I had was the spoon.

Why is it, the small part of me not engaged in the contemplation of violence wondered, *that I can listen to the ex-gays talk about the sin of homosexuality in the strongest possible language and not bat an eyelash, but that every word this man says about God makes me wish I had a butcher knife with me?* Then the words "butcher knife" opened up a new vista of fantasy and I was off again.

When David finally stopped talking, I began gathering my things to leave, but he wasn't done yet. "Do you mind if I pray?" he asked. I minded very much, but I had no idea how to say so. "O Father God," David said, and I knew I was doomed. "Thank You for Joel, thank You for his open mind and his open heart." I hated him so viciously I couldn't even bring myself to feel bad that he believed my mind and heart were open. "From our conversations I understand he wants to see You and wants to find You. So please reveal Yourself to him as You desire, and if I've said anything that isn't from You, please wipe it from his memory."

Unfortunately this did not happen. I remember every ex-cruciating detail.

When I got back to my room I called Mike and told him I had met an ex-gay Jew for Jesus, to which Mike replied, "Well, *he's* a joiner."

Every single person I met at the Exodus conference *loved* that I was a Jew. This was not because they believed, as many Jews fear evangelical Christians do, that the Jews' return to Israel will hasten the coming of the Antichrist and the end times. "I wish I could know the love Jesus has for you," said one woman I met. "You're one of the Chosen People!" She said this in the same awestruck tone of voice in which I might address some-body who had made it through week eight of *America's Next Top Model*.

The thing that seemed most difficult to grasp for a num-ber of the Exodus delegates—many of whom, as far as I could tell, had never met a Jewish person before—was the idea that we don't really pay attention to heaven or hell. "I mean, I think we might have an afterlife of some kind," I said one evening in conversation with very very handsome Matt, hot Jon's calendar-worthy friend from the First-Timers' Oasis, "but nobody ever talks about it." Upon my return to New York I did some research and discovered that we do in fact have hell, but it only lasts for a year, and then everybody goes to heaven.

"Then what's the point of obeying the Torah?" asked very very handsome Matt, pronouncing "Torah" very carefully, as if he feared I would report him to the Anti-Defamation League if he got it wrong.

"The point," I said, "is to be a good person here and now, not because you hope you'll be rewarded for it later on but because it's what you're supposed to do."

"Well, that doesn't make any sense to me," said very very handsome Matt. "If we didn't have an afterlife to worry about, I sure wouldn't be *here*. I'd be having group sex every night."

For the record, modern Jewish attitudes toward homosexuality differ as much as modern Christian attitudes. There are fundamentalist Israelis who have stabbed marchers in the Jerusalem Pride parade; there is a GLBT synagogue in Manhattan whose rabbi has been named (by three different national publications) one of America's top fifty Jewish leaders. When it comes to consistency, being the People of the Book doesn't give us any advantage over the goyim.

An old couple gave the testimony at the session after my dinner with David; they talked about their son Sean, who had rejected them after going into the lifestyle. "But we kept praying," said the mother, "and eventually he started to come around. He broke up with his lover, who was very dependent and needy. We got Sean to a therapist who had a good reputation for helping people change. But the night after he saw her for the first time, he was murdered by his ex-lover. The therapist called us the next day—she hadn't seen the morning paper—to say she thought Sean was ready to roll up his sleeves and get to work."

I shifted back and forth in my pew, unable to sit still. Every aspect of this story appalled me. The parents' misplaced hope, the homicidal lover, Sean's misplaced hope, the therapist's discussing her client with his family.

The father took over the narrative. "I was so angry at Sean," he said. "I was angry at all homosexuals. I said awful, terrible, hurtful things. And I pray every day for forgiveness for that." Someone from the audience shouted "You are forgiven!" and I was filled with a white-hot rage.

This is one element of Judaism on which I like to think I am crystal clear. You have to work *hard* to be forgiven. Every year on Yom Kippur, the Day of Atonement, Jews say the Kol Nidrei, asking God to pardon the sins we will commit against Him during the coming year. This prayer was written in Spain during the Inquisition, when the three choices open to Jews were to accept Jesus, to leave the country, or to burn. Those who feigned conversion to Christianity knew they would probably have to spend a lot of time eating pork or worshipping three gods or working on the Sabbath and decided to ask God to forgive these trespasses ahead of time in one fell swoop, annually.

But the Kol Nidrei applies only to sins we commit against God. To be forgiven for sins we commit against one another, we must follow a rigorous multistep process. Different descriptions offer different minutiae, but in the end you get something like this: First, after admitting that we have sinned, we have to feel remorse and resolve not to commit the sin again. Then we have to undo the damage we have done. And only then do we have the right to ask for forgiveness. If the person we wronged refuses to forgive us, then we have to go through the whole process over again, starting with admitting that we have sinned. And if the person we wronged refuses *again,* we have to do it all over again one more time. And if the answer is *still* no, then we're forgiven anyway, because he's being unreasonable. The only person who can forgive us is the person against whom we sinned; there can never be forgiveness from a third party. If the person we wronged is dead, we have to kneel at his grave and beg forgiveness in front of ten witnesses.

Forgiveness is *not easy* when you're a Jew.

I know this because of a letter my father sent me one Yom Kippur, when I was twenty-two, about how badly he and my mother had reacted when I came out. "I have never asked you for forgiveness," he wrote, after mentioning that he had just learned about the process of forgiveness in synagogue, "and I never could put my finger on why, except that I didn't feel entitled to yet. While I have been racked with enough pain to feel that I have been working on step 1, I also know that what I did to you has not yet been undone, so my wrong has not been repaired.

"And, in failing you, I failed Mom. Instead of passively following her lead and shrinking from arguing with her, I should have been struggling with her for your sake and for her sake, to help her do the right thing which I knew she could not do by herself.

"Perhaps the way I make it right to Mom is to help do what she can no longer do, which is to make it right to you— which is what I didn't do before, when I could have prevented so much of your pain."

I still have this letter; there are sections I can quote from memory. So when some bumpkin in the audience in Asheville called out, "You are forgiven!" I was consumed with a vast, unquenchable fire of hate. I hated them all: I hated the father, I hated the forgiver, I hated everyone in the room. I wanted to develop psychic powers and explode their heads. I wanted them all to burst into flames; I wanted them to die long, agonizing deaths full of suffering, starting right now. How *dared* they presume to forgive this man, how dared they rob that right from Sean or his spirit or his soul or whatever part of him hadn't rotted with his flesh? And how dared they forgive so cheaply? They didn't know what the man in front of them had said. They didn't know what he had done. They didn't know how his love or hatred or ignorance or understanding had shaped or misshaped his son or anyone else he knew. He felt remorse; that much was clear. But he had done nothing to make it right; instead, he had come here and applauded a thousand people for loathing themselves so much it made them sing. I didn't care that he felt this *was* making it right. Where was Sean's grave, that he might go to it and kneel down in front of ten witnesses and beg forgiveness for being grateful that at least his son didn't die gay? I wanted it to be Yom Kippur right now, so he could beg forgiveness of God, for believing Him to be so small-minded He gives a damn about who loves whom on this speck of dust.

And I hated myself for denying mercy to a grieving father. He had very clearly loved his son deeply even as he had probably fucked him up beyond all repair—well, now definitely beyond all repair, seeing as how he was lying in a box under the earth and would never be in a position to forgive anybody ever again.

On my way out of the session I felt a tap on my shoulder and turned around to see hot Jon, who looked unhappy. "I want to hear more about your story," he said.

"Fine," I said, "but are you all right?"

"Oh, I'm okay. It's just that last year I had such a wonderful experience at the conference, but so far this year I feel numb. I mean, if I'm here again and I'm not getting any new perspective on my life—well, it's a problem."

"That's rough."

"I look at my life, and I ask, am I happy? The first time I asked myself that was a year and a half ago, and I thought, damn it, I'm *not*. I mean, is this all there is? Make money, get rich, retire, live a life without joy?"

I didn't know what to say to this. For the first time, somebody I'd met here was expressing doubt. For the first time, somebody was saying he wasn't sure what his next step was.

Was this what they were all thinking?

"But I don't want to go on about myself," he said. "I want to hear more about you, why you came here."

This time Rob wasn't around to rescue me by telling us about the workshop he'd just been to. "I don't know," I said. "I just feel . . . an emptiness. Like, I wonder why I'm not filled with joy every time I see my boyfriend." I have not been filled with joy under any circumstances since I went off Prozac in 1999. But it would have been one thing to acknowledge that I had bad brain chemistry; to depict Mike as being a lesser part of my life than he actually was felt uncomfortably close to betrayal. I blamed Jon for this, and I suddenly realized he was incredibly annoying.

And he wouldn't let it go. He kept on asking questions. He asked about my boyfriend. He asked about my experience in the lifestyle. He asked about my childhood, and I talked about how my father had worked a lot and I had had to take care of my dying mother and I couldn't complain because he was off saving the world. I talked and talked and talked. I did not wish to say the things I said to him, because they were true and because they were not things I felt comfortable revealing, but I was unable to make anything up. By now I found him extraordinarily unattractive. The more strongly he expressed sympathy the more adamantly I refused to let it move me. I apologized for talking so much, when in fact I was furious at him for making me do so.

Finally—*finally*—I was able to wrench the conversation around to him, and he revealed that, after the Exodus conference the previous year, he had walked out on Stacey on her birthday and spent the rest of the day in a gay sex club. Eventually, however, he had realized that the lifestyle was miserable and that he belonged with his wife.

"And now things are amazing," he said. "I mean, okay, I've never gotten an erection looking at her, or at any woman. So when we have sex, we turn the lights off, she touches me, she scratches my back, and that's how we start. No, it's not the same excitement I get from sex with a man. But it's so wonderful to wake up next to someone you trust and who trusts you and hear your seven-year-old daughter and your twin sons laughing, who love each other so much, and you."

*Your **daughter**? I thought. Your **sons**? You have **children**? I just met you, and I can see your marriage imploding before my eyes. What were you thinking?*

"There's one guy here," he said, "who really triggers me. I told Stacey, and she said, what are you going to do about it? I said, I'm gonna get to know him. And I went and spent a long time talking with him. He told me all about his life, and I'm like, Whoa, you have some serious stuff going on. You have problems just like me. And I don't feel inferior to him anymore."

Fuck.

He was talking about me.

He had sought me out, without his wife. He had made a big deal of being interested in my story. All that insistence on finding out what was missing from my life—he hadn't been grilling me; he had really wanted to know. He had needed to find something wrong with me so that he could keep believing that to be happy he had to be straight.

What damage had I done him by shoring up that belief?

The next afternoon Rob invited me and Jon to go swimming with him in the Asheville River Jon declined, saying that he and Stacey wanted to go to the local crafts fair, but I was all for the idea of taking my clothes off in front of Rob. Unfortunately, before we left he acquired three other companions—Bill, the cute, bubbly twink; Louis, the hairdresser with bad hair; and Greg, the sullen deaf guy. But something about the river eased my spirits, and before long I was jumping from the log that hung from the tree, Wicked Witch of the West or no, and swimming back to shore, laughing the whole time.

And for the first time since the start of the conference, I didn't feel like a con man. I don't know whether it was the absence of a notebook that did it, or the fact that nobody was discussing brokenness or healing or father wounds, or the fact that I couldn't see a goddamned thing because I didn't have my contacts in, but I could almost feel my innards untwisting themselves.

I attempted a back somersault off the log, landed on my back, and got water up my nose, but I tried again and this time I went in upright. Bill followed my lead; Rob started to but he was too muscular to pull his knees far enough into his chest for a somersault. Louis was well built too—and well tanned, though his bronzed palms gave him away as a user of self-tanning cream—but he was sitting on a rock on the shore, not swimming.

I stood with Rob knee-deep in the water near the bank and talked with him and Louis. I kept losing my balance, but I was not sorry to have to reach out repeatedly and grab Rob's arm to steady myself. *Is he into me?* I wondered, and couldn't tell. I am an unskilled interpreter of nonverbal clues in even the clearest of circumstances; in murkier situations, when the people around me are stifling all their impulses, I feel moorless; and in murkier situations when the people around me are stifling all their impulses and my vision is not corrected I might as well be clutching jetsam on the high seas. So in order to see whether Rob was indeed into me I climbed out of the river to put on my glasses, but when I did so everything came into sharp focus again, and I instantly felt severed from human connection with the four men fifty feet away from me. I had forgotten for a quarter of an hour that I was an outsider, and, now that I remembered, the feeling was excruciating. *If this is what clear vision costs,* I thought, *I prefer not to see.* I put my glasses back in my sneaker and climbed once more onto the rock.

Forty-five minutes later, dry and clothed, we headed back to the car, where we stood around uncomfortably; something didn't seem quite right. Then Rob pulled a bottle of hair gel out of his bag and we all took some and everything was okay again. Rob and I walked along the river; twenty sullen feet ahead of us was Greg, with Bill and Louis in front of him. "Greg is frustrated with me," said Rob. "I think he's attracted to me, and that's not what I'm here for. He wanted to touch my leg in the car."

"What'd you do?" I asked, willing Greg to fall into the river and drown.

"I just moved it away." Okay, Greg could stay alive.

I mean, it's not as if I would actually have done anything with Rob had the opportunity presented itself. First, it would totally have fucked him up even further; and second, I already had a boyfriend, one who had no wish to be free from his homosexuality through the power of Jesus Christ, one who could write me prescriptions for benzodiazepines.

"We'll be there in a second," Rob called to Bill, Louis, and Greg, who had returned to the car. Looking at me, he said, "What are your plans for when you go back?"

A flash of inspiration struck me. "I don't think I'm going to try to change. But when I get back home, I'm going to be faithful to my boyfriend. I'm going to treat him better. I'm going to be a better person." This, I realized, would be the end of the story I told the people here. And maybe by giving them an example of someone who had made a different choice, someone who didn't hate himself—or at least who didn't hate himself for being gay—I could at least keep questions open in their minds.

"But how long is that going to last?"

"We'll see." I wasn't sure I felt comfortable with where I thought this was heading.

"I'll be honest with you," he said. "You're smart, you're personable, and I think you deserve more." *You left out cute, I* thought petulantly. "My skin may want a man," he said, "but inside I just want total intimacy." *The two propositions are not mutually exclusive!* I wanted to scream at him. "I want everything for you, great relationships with men *and* women. When you say those words, *my boyfriend*—well, it just . . . it doesn't fit." Disappointment bloomed in me. *I was going to rescue him,* I thought, *and instead he's trying to rescue me.* But neither one of us was interested in being rescued.

In the car on the way back to the conference center, Rob asked Louis, "How do you see yourself as a man?" Louis looked perplexed. "I mean," Rob explained, "are there ways in which you see yourself as not measuring up to what you think of as a man?"

"My career," Louis said. "I missed the boat by not going to college, and now it's too late. I only became a hairdresser because my wife was one. And she was better than me. We got divorced a couple years ago and it was horrible. I'm selling my condo at a loss to meet the settlement terms. All those messages I was checking earlier were from my realtor."

Somehow he had begun to seem less annoying.

After Rob parked, Louis and I walked back together to our rooms. "I wanted to jump into the river," he said suddenly. "But I had an accident when I was a kid and almost drowned. Ever since then I've been scared of the water."

"We would have saved you," I said.

"I heard somebody drowned in that river three days ago. Not unless you'd all ranged yourselves across the river to catch me. I could have done it then."

"Next time," I promised him fiercely, wondering whether he would ever be in a position to take this chance again, and hating God for allowing life to lacerate a person so.

Later that night I saw hot Jon talking to very very handsome Matt. They were discussing gym regimens. "The conference has been hard for me," said very very handsome Matt. "My head has been full of defiling thoughts, and I've had a hard heart."

Realization hit me in the face like a mud patty: It was Matt to whom Jon was attracted, not me. It was Matt who triggered him. It was Matt he had told his wife about and sought out and talked to for a long time.

I instantly lost the remaining shred of interest I had in Jon and went to the ice-cream parlor, where I was propositioned by a sizzling ex-gay standing in front of me in line. ("What would you do if you had the chance to take somebody back to your room?" he asked me, staring me in the eyes as he licked his butter pecan ice cream. I did not take him up on his offer. My boyfriend fucking *owes* me.)

Everybody at the conference seemed to take as a given that homosexuality is spiritually and physically harmful both to those who practice it and to those around them. "If I go back just once, I could get AIDS," Vito had said.

What about a CONDOM? I had wanted to shriek. *What about SAFE SEX? What about THE FACT THAT STRAIGHT PEOPLE CAN GET HIV?* When I got back from the conference I figured I might as well check my facts. International data on transmission mechanisms turned out to be appallingly sparse, but in every report I could find the majority of HIV infections were linked to something other than gay sex. If AIDS is a punishment, I wanted to ask—very few people came out and said this but it was implied in every discussion of HIV—then why are you here instead of starting a conference to help black women in southern Africa turn white and move to Newark?

Another assumption at the conference, voiced more frequently than the AIDS-as-punishment idea but never examined closely, was that gay couples are incapable of monogamy. I researched this too when I got back to New York, and though different studies gave numbers all over the place, the ones that seemed most methodologically sound suggested that about a third of gay couples choose to have open relationships, a third pledge monogamy but one partner or the other cheats, and a third pledge monogamy and stick to it. This means that, of gay couples claiming to be monogamous (two-thirds of all gay couples), half of them actually are.

Which, surprise surprise, is the same figure suggested by studies of straight married couples.

"But aren't all gay couples non-monogamous?" Louis asked me at one point. "That's what I've heard."

"No," I said, exasperated. "A lot of couples I know aren't monogamous, but a lot of them are." It was obvious he didn't believe me. "Look," I said crossly, "I'll make a list." I pulled out my notebook to make a table of gay couples I knew and whether they were monogamous or not. Since I write musicals and everyone I know is gay, this should have been easy, but under pressure I was unable to think of more than five homosexuals personally known to me. In the end I just made up couples and monogamy statuses. My fake list looked like this:

John & Michael	Y
Stephen & Michael	N
Robert & Aaron	Y
Jay & Jeff	Y
Tim & Whatshisname	N

Keith & Jim	N
Daniel & Joey	Y
Christopher & Bill	N
James & Jon	N
Michael & Toby	Y
Kenny & Tom	Y

"See?" I said, showing Louis the list. "Out of eleven couples, seven say they're monogamous, which means that statistically three or four of them are." I do not know a Keith & Jim or a Michael & Toby or, in fact, most of the couples on this list. When in the quiet of my room I calmed down enough to remember gay couples I knew and with whom I had talked about monogamy, I found that my numbers had been pretty much on the mark.

⟶

"I'm sad to leave," said Rob as I peppered my chicken fingers during lunch on the last day of the conference. I was relieved to be eating, as I had just attended a workshop at which a woman in her sixties had suggested to a roomful of men that when we felt the urge to masturbate we could keep ourselves from doing so by singing "There's Power in the Blood," which I happened to know was a particularly gruesome Baptist hymn. "It's impossible to abuse yourself," she had said, "when you're singing about the power of Jesus." My mind had filled instantly with a picture of gay men all over America jacking off while singing "There's Power in the Blood," and since then I had felt somewhat light-headed.

"This isn't the real world," Rob continued. "A lot of guys don't have people at home who know they're struggling, and this is the one place they can be honest about who they are. A lot of guys get rejected by their churches if they're truthful. People who say they're Christians can really be hypocrites. They go to church just like they're supposed to and put on a mask, but then the rest of the week they go and do everything everybody else does who isn't Christian."

I was so horrified by the idea that this was as open as the ex-gays got that I couldn't say anything for a moment. Then Louis came over and asked if he could join us; I wanted to throw my chocolate milk in his face—how could Rob fall in love with me if he never got to spend any time alone with me?—but instead I nodded and said sure.

The conference had been wonderful, said Louis sadly, and he didn't want to go home the next day. "I feel like I'm just at the beginning of my pain. That means I'm also at the beginning of showing God my pain, but that doesn't make it easy." His ex-wife had turned his church against him, he said, and the next church he joined had expelled him for getting divorced. Now he went to yet another church, where a few people knew he was struggling.

"I just have so little confidence in myself," said Louis.

Rob assured him that we all have problems with self-confidence. "I feel like less of a man," he said, "around guys who talk about changing engines or hunting or the ball game. When I was little I was just like that guy in Monty Python who says, I just want to sing! I just wanted to dance. I took three years of lessons. Jazz, tap, ballet. But I stopped because my dad said dancing was for sissies. Now I wish I'd kept it up."

"Show us some moves!" I said.

He smiled. "That was a long time ago."

Louis was gazing at Rob, haunted, his eyes hollow, his cheeks sunken. He couldn't be devoid of hope; otherwise he wouldn't be here. But I had never seen anybody who seemed to believe less that his life would get any better. I wanted to cry. "Are you ever attracted to women?" he asked Rob suddenly.

"I wish I were," Rob said, "but I'm not. And I'm thirty-eight. Getting from where I am now to married with children seems like a really long journey."

"But God will do it in His own time," said Louis, "if you trust Him. He can do it in a day." He went on to talk about how sex with a woman was beautiful. "But I wish I had hotter chemistry with women," he said. "To get aroused with a woman I need her to rub my back, massage my shoulders, stuff like that. Although when I initiate things it's easier for me to get aroused."

Rob turned to me. "How's sex with your boyfriend?"

I almost choked on my chocolate milk. "It's actually really good," I said once I had recovered my composure. "We fit together really well. I'm not sure if I should say this while we're eating, but—oh, I'll just go ahead. When we have sex I'm generally the receptive one, and he's the penetrative one, and—"

"Is that, um, a top?"

I laughed. "Yes, that's a top. Top and bottom."

"I just learned those words two days ago," Rob said proudly.

"I learned them a couple months ago, off the Internet," said Louis.

"I don't understand you," Rob said to me, and went on, mercifully releasing me from the obligation to wax lyrical about the joys of coitus with Mike in between bites of chicken fingers. "What I can't wrap my little limited mind around is: I came here last year, and I had wrestled for months and months and had all kinds of conversations with all kinds of people. It was a big deal for me to come. You, you're Jewish, you haven't thought about any of this before, you're in the lifestyle, you're staying in the lifestyle. I don't get it. Why did you come here?"

I was standing on treacherous ground. I stammered, "I, I, I think that, uh, that some of the things you're, um, talking about actually make it...um...easier for me rather than harder. I knew this was a Christian organization and that there would be a lot of stuff that just didn't make sense for me. So that took the pressure off. Also, um, I've had a good experience with the gay lifestyle, so, uh, so I didn't have the sense that what I was coming to *had* to work, or else."

Rob could see as clearly as I could that this made no sense. "Yeah, but it's expensive to come here. You could have just read an article."

"I did," I choked out, "but I wanted to see it for real, come and understand what this is about."

"What *what* is about?" asked Rob, frustrated.

This was getting worse and worse. I changed the subject slightly, hoping he wouldn't notice, and offered something about being dissatisfied with my own behavior and finding the testimonies really inspiring and—

"I feel like I can't give a testimony," said Louis. I could have kissed him for rescuing me. "I've made so little progress on the journey out of homosexuality." Rob said he felt the same way, and Louis looked at him strangely. "But your testimony would bless so many people."

"Why?"

"Because of the way you look," said Louis, coming as close as he could to "because you're totally hot."

"But you're here at an Exodus conference," said Rob. "You've gotten somewhere. I haven't had any huge victories either. But it's the direction that's important."

The nap into which I fell immediately upon returning to my room proved afterward to be a mistake, since I always wake up from naps depressed. I rubbed the sleep from my eyes and started watching the first episode of season two of *The West Wing* (which I had also brought with me, in case the eighties clothing in *The Twilight Zone* got to be too much) and when I saw that it was Josh who had been shot in the first season finale I burst into uncontrollable sobs. Who the fuck did I think I was? What gave me the right to stop asking questions and pretend to find my own answers? I had come to care about these people more than I had imagined possible, and what ruinous things had I said to them? How dared I?

I called Mike, barely intelligible through my tears. "I came here as a jo-o-oke," I wailed. "And I'm doing it. I'm playing a joke with these people's souls." My breath heaved. "What kind of da-a-a-amage am I doing to them?"

"People are resilient," Mike said. "You can't do that much damage in four days."

"I, I, I can't?" Snot dripped from my nose.

"No," he said. "And you also can't save them in four days."

"But I can try!"

"No."

I sniffled and wished that what he'd just said weren't true.

We kept talking and I gradually calmed down. "I was worried this would happen," he said.

My eyes narrowed. "Did you *predict* this?"

"No," he said. "I thought it would go the other way—that they would be really negative and you would feel alienated. But this is worse, because the negative energy is self-directed, and you're empathizing with them."

After we hung up I realized that I could have come to the Exodus conference and been completely honest with the people I met. "I'm gay," I could have said, "and I'm here because I don't see why anybody would want to change, or even think it's possible, and I just want to understand more." And they would have welcomed me with open arms.

I felt as if I were in a teen movie, the photographic negative of the kind in which the guy pretends to be gay to get close to the girl, and *does* get close to the girl, but then has to confess to her that he's actually straight. In the movies, this confession always goes over very well, and they end up together.

In real life things might be a bit more complicated.

As Rob, Louis, and I entered the auditorium for the final evening session, the man onstage was saying, "God, I believe there's at least one person in this room whose heart is still hard. And I pray that You would soften it." *Already done,* I thought ruefully.

"Here," said Rob, handing me a plastic bag. "We got this

for you." Inside was a DVD of *The Ballad of Little Joe,* an ani-
mated Veggie Tales version of Joseph and the Coat of Many
Colors, with vegetables, as a Western (Joseph was a cucumber
and the brothers were green peas); there was also a pack of
Veggie Tales cards.

"Thank you," I said, feeling deeply moved and hating myself and wanting Rob to bend me over the pew and take me,
all at the same time.

The evening's testimony and service were exactly like all
the other testimonies and services. At the end, I went up
toward the front to ask the prayer team for help. I felt foul, and
I wanted to be pardoned before I left. This time I didn't run
away. When my turn came I was led to a short, stout older
woman in a floral-print dress. "Thank you," I said, and
grabbed her hand and started crying. I told her my name and
she said, "Thank you for you, Joel. God, I pray that You let Joel
know there is an army of angels protecting him, and he doesn't
have to do this alone." I wished more than anything that I
could believe this.

On my way up the aisle I had expected to be filled with the
urge to confess and to beg forgiveness for what I was doing,
but instead as she continued to pray she just made me feel nice.

As I came back to my seat in between Rob and Louis, the
man onstage said, "I pray that those who are frozen with fear
would get the strength to come up to the front and pray." I felt
that Louis, who had not moved a muscle, might be among the
frozen. He was leaving tomorrow, to go back to a life in which
he had to deal with his ex-wife and his career dissatisfaction and
his bad hair, with selling his condo at a loss, with not knowing
anybody like him. The bond these people felt with one another
may have been dysfunctional, but they were part of a community all the same, and that community was about to be rent asun-

der. I put my hand on Louis's neck and kept it there. He started crying, or maybe he'd already been crying and he was just more obvious about it now. After a while Rob put his head down in his arms. I couldn't tell whether he was crying or not. I put my hand on his back and held it there. I asked whatever forces there might be in the universe to have mercy on the three of us, and on everybody in the room. *If there's any way for my goodwill to help these two men,* I thought, *then let it help them.*

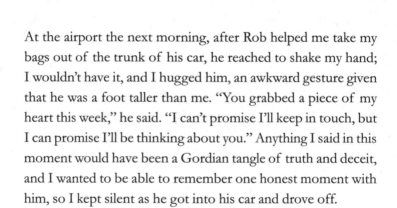

At the airport the next morning, after Rob helped me take my bags out of the trunk of his car, he reached to shake my hand; I wouldn't have it, and I hugged him, an awkward gesture given that he was a foot taller than me. "You grabbed a piece of my heart this week," he said. "I can't promise I'll keep in touch, but I can promise I'll be thinking about you." Anything I said in this moment would have been a Gordian tangle of truth and deceit, and I wanted to be able to remember one honest moment with him, so I kept silent as he got into his car and drove off.

I had always thought that the Christian right was motivated by selfishness, intolerance, and fear. But the story, as I mused on the plane ride home, isn't that simple. The Christian right—or at least the thousand members of it at the conference—or at least the half dozen of them I got to know decently—they don't hate gay people; in fact they can be more consistently thoughtful and generous than many of the crowds that might be found in a gay bar on a Saturday night. Oh, I won't mount any defense of Pat Robertson or James Dobson or the venal politicians who find it expedient to stand with them, and I won't deny that a lot of people in this country are afraid of people who seem different. But I think most of the Christian conservatives on the street don't want us to go to hell. They want to save us from danger. Their reaction against gay-rights legislation is an altruistic one. If I ran a zoo, and somebody came to me and said, "Hey, I have a great idea! Let's take down the walls around the shark pool so all the kids can swim with the sharks!" I would have him thrown out on his ass. To many of these people, laws that make it easier to be gay only give Satan freer access to our souls.

And I don't know how the two sides, acting in good faith, can ever reach an agreement, because it comes down to whether God said so or not. And if you believe that God said man shall not lie with mankind as with a woman, it is an abomination, well, then no amount of argument is going to change your mind. And if you believe that God doesn't interfere on such a microscopic level with humanity, or that He doesn't give a fuck about us, or that He has never existed at all, then nothing is going to convince you that if you disobey Him you are bound for the Pit.

I had foolishly given my e-mail address to my swimming companions, and two days after my return to Manhattan I got a message from Rob, informing me that I was a cool guy, that he thought he could learn a lot from me, and that he was impressed with my openness and honesty.

Two days later I got a message from Bill hoping my trip home had been safe.

Three days after that I got a message from Louis saying he didn't want to lose track of me.

These e-mails sat in my in-box for weeks, torturing me in twelve-point Helvetica type. On the one hand, I wanted to stay in touch with Rob and Bill and Louis, so I could show them that they had options. I fantasized about a growing intimacy with them, an intimacy that led to New York visits during which they spent time with me and Mike and realized they could be gay *and* happy, visits during which they broke free of the chains with which they had allowed themselves to be shackled.

But I always ran up against the fact that any good such an example might do them would be destroyed utterly when my book was published and they read it and they found out that I had been deceiving them all along. "I lied to people to make them like me," I moaned to my friend Sarah.

"We ALL lie to people to make them like us," she shouted in frustration.

Except that I had also unintentionally infused my conference interactions with a great deal of truth. Yes, I was practicing a deception. But in the end I did show them who I was, and I did come to care about them deeply. How was jumping out over the Asheville River a lie? How was putting my hand on Louis's neck when he was weeping a lie? How was laughing a lie?

I wished I had never given any of them my e-mail address. I called my father for advice five times a day. I talked to my therapist about the issue and found him singularly unhelpful, so I got a new therapist, who was no better. I ordered a copy of Sissela Bok's *Lying* but it got lost in the mail.

I still haven't answered the e-mails.

That, more or less, is what I wrote during the summer after I got back from the Exodus Freedom Conference, and I thought it was the end of the story.

It wasn't.

A few weeks after I finished a first draft, Rob e-mailed me again to tell me he had found my website and read about my book, *Gay Haiku*. "Imagine me, knowing a famous author," he wrote. "If you write a play about the crazy Exodus crowd, please get a good actor to play me."

"The game is over," said Mike when I showed him Rob's e-mail. "He knows why you were there." Something frozen in me began to melt.

"It was great to get to know you in Asheville," I wrote back. "I may just write something about the Exodus crowd. And I'll get Tom Cruise to play you." I attached a photograph of myself playing softball at the gay summer camp from which I had just returned. "Let me know if you're ever in New York and I'll show you the town."

"Sorry, brother," he responded, "but you just don't seem very 'gay' to me. You did not have any fear of the water in NC and were quite daring on that rope swing. Now you send me a picture of you looking like a natural at home plate." I did not tell him that I looked like a natural only because a lesbian had adjusted my stance.

As Rob and I continued our intercontinental correspondence, I made sure to include subtle references to my boyfriend and our life together, to keep before him the idea that it might be possible for a gay person to find intimacy at places other than rest stops. "Don't be too aggressive with him," warned Mike. "You don't want him to shut down."

Rob sent me a frustrated e-mail about a doctor in Cádiz he'd become friends with who wanted to be more than friends, and I sent him a supportive response. He wrote back, "I wish I could give you a big hug right now!" *He totally has a crush on me,* I thought.

I told Mike to watch his step. "There's a guy in Spain who'd be *happy* to wash the dishes if I asked him to," I said.

But as the months went by it began to dawn on me that Rob really *didn't* know I had been undercover at the conference. I was once again tortured by guilt but this time the decision was much easier to make; I had maintained an emotional bond with him, and I owed him the truth. I dropped an off-hand remark into a subordinate clause in my next e-mail that left no room for doubt ("Since I'm sure you've figured out by now that I was at the conference doing research for a book . . .").

He didn't answer.

He still didn't answer.

He continued not to answer.

"I'm not sure what you're feeling about me," I wrote finally, my fingers trembling, "but if we aren't in touch again I just want to tell you that in the short time we spent together I grew to admire you deeply."

His response came almost immediately. "Lighten up, my friend," he wrote. "My silence only means that I'm overworked. You did a great spy job. I was honest when I said that you have a piece of my heart. And through our e-mails that piece has stayed alive." He wrote a little bit more about Jesus and ended with, "Keep searching for Truth."

I burst into tears in the middle of Starbucks.

We stayed in touch, and in April he told me his summer traveling schedule had him laying over in New York for a few days in July, so naturally I insisted that he stay with us. I joked to Mike about how excited I was to realize my conversion fantasy. I started planning menus; I investigated various tours of the city; I bought tickets to *Wicked,* the Broadway musical that tells a different *Wizard of Oz* story, in which Glinda and the Wicked Witch of the West start out as school roommates and best friends. "If a musical about the Wicked Witch of the West doesn't turn him gay," I said, "then nothing will."

He arrived and hung out with us. We went to my favorite Thai restaurant. He came to the gym with me. I cooked chicken with pineapple-jalapeño salsa, and peach Melba for dessert. We got caught in a downpour. We went to Central Park and took photographs. He asked my advice about the doctor in Cádiz; I told him he didn't have to stay friends with this guy just to be nice. He told me he had been in touch with Louis, who was now back in the lifestyle and had a boyfriend, something I was very happy to hear. I asked Rob if he believed that people who don't believe in Jesus are going to hell, and he said that, if they've had the opportunity to believe and chosen not to, then yes, they're going to hell. I asked if that included me and he said no, Jews are a special case.

Then, the night before he left, we went to the theater. I had seen *Wicked* before, and I was looking forward to sharing it with Rob. Even if he didn't want to be gay, I thought, how could he not love a show that portrays the Wicked Witch of the West as a spunky young heroine (named Elphaba) who meets the Wizard, realizes he is waging a perfidious war against the citizens of Oz, and sets herself against him with a power she has barely begun to understand?

Just as I had expected, Rob was mesmerized by the spiky

Swish

Elphaba and her sparkling rival Glinda. I realize now that I was watching with only half my mind; the other half was reeling with metaphor. Some of it I had expected. We were watching a show about a character who was not like other people and shunned because of it; a character who, after spending much of her adolescence hoping to fit in with everybody else, decided to accept herself for who she was; a character who, hidden behind a black hat and a broomstick and a mask of green skin, found the freedom to choose for herself who she wanted to be. This was the archetype of the coming-out tale—whether gay or ex-gay, anybody in our society who has felt homosexual attractions knows how the story goes. Hell, anybody in our society who has felt *different* knows how the story goes. My decision to dress as a witch for Hallowe'en at age five had been wiser than I knew.

What I hadn't expected upon walking into the theater, though, was that I would see my friendship with Rob reflected in the friendship between the two witches onstage. Of course there was the obvious: from vastly different backgrounds, with vastly different self-images, heading in vastly different directions, they forged nonetheless a bond as real as it was unlikely. But as I watched them struggle, Glinda against the seductive safety of being loved, Elphaba against the small-mindedness of those around her; as I watched them yearn, Glinda to be good, Elphaba to belong; as I watched them fail, Glinda for lack of courage, Elphaba for lack of facility, I grew less and less able to figure out which one of them was Rob and which one of them was me.

When the two girls barricaded themselves in a tower against the Wizard's guards, however, I abandoned the attempt, because we had almost reached the act-one finale, to my mind the high point of the show. Glinda urged her friend to apologize to the Wizard so everything would be okay again, but Elphaba responded that something had changed in her, that she knew it was time to leap. "I think I'll try defying gravity," she sang, and kept on singing. And then, in the middle of the song, for one exhilarating moment, Glinda seemed on the verge of joining Elphaba in the quest to bring freedom to the land of Oz and to seize a share in that freedom. The witches' hands gripped Elphaba's broomstick as if they belonged to one woman.

And then the energy onstage shifted, and Glinda stepped back. "I hope you're happy, now that you're choosing this," she sang, and her best friend answered, "You, too." The Wizard's men broke into the room; Glinda rushed to block their way but they pushed roughly past her. It didn't matter, though, because the girl who would become the Wicked Witch of the West had begun, for the first time, to fly. Swathed in billowing midnight, soaring higher and higher above the stage, as Glinda and the Wizard's soldiers looked up in awe, she sang that if they cared to find her they should look to the western sky. "I'm flying high, defying gravity!" she exulted, and then her melody became wordless and from high above us her voluminous black robe spread and spread until its eldritch shadow covered the entire stage and the audience's applause exploded before the curtain had even begun to fall.

"So?" I said, turning to Rob and wiping my eyes as the houselights came up. "What do you think?"

"Wow," he said, "this is amazing. What a way to pop my Broadway cherry." I laughed. "They have great voices. If I get the CD out in the lobby, will it be these people singing?"

"No. But the people on the CD will be just as good, if not better."

"Back in Cádiz," said Rob, segueing into some anecdote

about his next-door neighbor that had nothing to do with witches or Oz or homosexuality, and I felt a rush of disappointment that I had to work very hard to keep off my face.

And then it hit me: My line to Mike about the Wicked Witch of the West turning Rob gay had been only mostly a joke. Some very small part of me had really thought that, when Rob saw Elphaba rise from the ground, singing "It's time to try defying gravity," he would smack his forehead, turn to me, and say, *"Now* I see the truth!" Faced with incontrovertible proof of my point of view, he would have to surrender; he would abandon his narrow idea of God and become more than he had ever imagined he could be.

But we weren't in my own personal dimension, we were in the Gershwin Theatre on Fifty-first Street; and this wasn't Purim, it was a regular day, neither Mordecai nor Esther in sight; and Rob had reacted to the enjoyable spectacle before him with, well, enjoyment. I already knew how the show ended: the witches' friendship changed both of them for the better, but Elphaba stayed wicked and Glinda stayed good, whatever those words meant in the version of the world onstage in front of us.

I had wanted to rescue Rob at the theater just as he had wanted to rescue me at the Exodus conference. But now I think that in fact neither one of us *can* be rescued. If he comes to think differently about his sexuality, it will not be because of anything I have said or done; he will simply have come to think differently about the universe and our place in it. The same goes for me: I cannot say for certain that I will never believe in Jesus—after all, I once said I would never end a sentence with a preposition or wear rayon—but I'm pretty sure it would take more than a weekend visit to a friend to do the trick. Every one of us is lost in a different way, and the only one who can save

Rob is Rob, and the only one who can save Jon is Jon, and the only one who can save me is me. As we stumble around searching for Truth, the best we can do is to remind one another, when we collide, that there are moments in which we are not alone.

"Hey, should we go get some snacks?" I asked Rob as we sat in the theater.

"Sure," he said, and we went out into the lobby and stood together eating M&M's until it was time to go back in for the second act.

$\mathcal{A}$CKNOWLEDGMENTS

My first thanks must go to Joy Tutela, the sexiest agent in New York, to David Black, the second-sexiest agent in New York, and to Andrew Corbin, the sexiest editor in New York, for their faith in this book and in me. If you've enjoyed what you've read, it is to them and to the sexiest assistants in New York, John Burke, David Larabell, Darya Porat, and Johnathan Wilber, that you owe your thanks.

Without Sarah Rose, precious adviser, colleague, and friend, this book wouldn't exist.

Without Victoria Cain, *I* probably wouldn't exist.

Bob Alpert, Jon Barrett, David Buscher, John Crook, Rob Hartmann, Phil Higgins, Andy McQuery, Pamela Merritt, John Morgan, Dan Rhatigan, Julia Sullivan, Jennifer Tattenbaum, Greg Yoder, and the members of the Sackett Street Writers Non-Fiction Workshop (www.sackettworkshop.com), Ryan Carrasco, Abigail Carroll, Beth Cranwell, Jessica DuLong, Beth Greenfield, Emily Helfgot, Lori Hurley, Laura Longhine, Maureen Miller, Helen Newman, Liz Skillman, and Samantha Walters, gave me invaluable critiques on what they read and forgave me for hating their guts when they didn't tell me everything was already perfect. I owe a particular debt of gratitude to Lauren Naturale, whose patience is as everlasting as her insight is keen, and to Nancy Rawlinson (www.nancyrawlinson.

com), who knew not only exactly what the writing needed but also exactly how to tell me.

Without the behind-the-scenes work of Ruth Childs, Bob de Luna, Chris Keane, Erik Liberman, Anya Nawrocky, Matthew Phillp, and Veronica Vera of Miss Vera's Finishing School for Boys Who Want to Be Girls, many of the pages between these covers would be blank.

Ted Conover provided excellent ethical advice at the right moment. Tommy Semosh provided excellent advice on both publicity and facial hair.

If *Swish* is not riddled with errors when it veers from its main subject—that is to say, me—it is because of Michael Bailey, Michael Bussee, Gene McAfee, Noam Pianko, Robert Spitzer, Warren Throckmorton, and Dean Wendt.

I must thank Steven Best, Alfred Kleinbaum, Jonathan Portera, Cheryl Whaley, and Eric Wolff for keeping me sane, literally.

I feel especially grateful to those who played central roles in the stories I've told: Glenn Bassett, Susan Clinkenbeard, Bill Cole, Sasha Derfner, Gina Fried, Andrew Jonas, Holly Lisanby, Antonio Montovani, Oscar Morales, Daniel Nardicio, Kerry Riffle, and Jonathan Vatner. I owe a particular debt to the men and women I met at the Exodus, International Freedom Conference. I hope they find the peace they are looking for.

My brother Jeremy was there when I started and, though he's moved across the continent, he has supported me the whole time as if he were still living twenty feet away from me. Though I have forbidden my father, Armand, to read most of the chapters, he and his wife Mary—along with my in-laws, Ken, Ronnie, Cathy, and Dennis—have been more enthusiastic than I could ever have hoped for. Unfortunately my mother,

Mary Frances, left this earth before I began writing, but her spirit infuses every page.

Mindi Dickstein, Len Schiff, Rachel Sheinkin, and Peter Ullian have not only taught me most of what I know about writing but also displayed extraordinary patience with the number of projects I've insisted on juggling

Fred Carl, Marie Costanza, Julianne Davis, Martin Epstein, Sean Flahaven, Karen Henderson, Danny Larsen, Robert Lee, Mel Marvin, Sybille Pearson, Sarah Schlesinger, Alex Zalben, and the Graduate Musical Theater Writing Program at NYU have given me a home.

And last, and most, I want to thank Mike Combs, for more than I can ever say.